OVER THE DOORSTEP

Over the Doorstep

by

RITA F. SNOWDEN

*'The Lord will keep your going out
and your coming in...'* Psalm 121–8, *R.S.V.*

LONDON
EPWORTH PRESS

SET IN MONOTYPE BASKERVILLE AND PRINTED IN
GREAT BRITAIN BY NEILL AND CO LTD PRINTERS
EDINBURGH

To

MARJORIE STEWART

*How much richer life became when I
stepped over your doorstep, and you over mine!*

Introduction

This book begins where we are—because the promise on which it is based belongs where we are.

Our doorstep of 'West Hills' is comparatively new; yours may be worn hollow with the passing of feet. But it makes no difference: 'The Lord will keep your going out, and your coming in . . .'

On one side of our doorstep life is shared with the few—spelling out our most personal and sacred obligations. On the other side is the great world—greater by far than any before us have imagined it.

To pass 'over the doorstep' was a simple thing once—the shepherd to his tiny flock; the farmer of a later century to his tilling; later still, the bread-winner to his desk or his little store. Women-folk had then no thought of spending hours out of the home, save for social calling.

Now all is changed with the changed world in which we find ourselves. A bloodless revolution has taken place with the coming of the combustion-engine, electricity and the advantages and threats of nuclear power. Tastes expand with incomes, wants become needs. From the circle of those most dear, we go out into a world of business and bustle, where often the values that make life good are little recognized. Our battle is not alone for bread, but to keep alive the truth that man does not live by bread alone. We are at the mercy of many new factors—from microbes to drunken drivers, from mistaken judgements of politicians to the possibility of bombs dropped on our heads.

Mercifully, on both sides of the doorstep is the blessing of God—as real as any of these other realities—keeping us in our going out and our coming in.

R.F.S.

All—Always

I STOOD waiting a turn at the stamp-counter of our tiny post-office this morning with a bank-note in my hand. The man being served as I entered wanted three air-mail stamps and two four-pennies; the woman coming next, eight penny ones. But this kind of niggly buying leaves my stamp-box continually empty. As I gave my order, the post-mistress reached under the counter for an untorn page of stamps. Stepping out of the queue—my needs supplied—I suddenly thought of Sir Herbert Beerbohm Tree, the famous actor. He once went into a post-office to buy a stamp. The clerk brought out a sheet of one hundred stamps, and Tree studied it very carefully. Finally, he pointed to the centre of the sheet, and said, 'I'll take that one'. (I know you'd like to hear what the postal clerk said; but I'm not telling.)

Was the matter as a whole more ridiculous than that of one who will—so to speak, point out a situation, and say, 'I'll make that a religious issue?' Surely, if there is a matter in the middle of the day's doings worth praying about, then the whole of it must be. No single issue can be isolated; either the whole of life is religious or it is secular. Preparation for church-membership, or the sickness of a member of the family, is no more a subject for religion, than answering the telephone at the office, or sweeping the stair at home. Angela Morgan states this arrestingly. She says:

> As I go commonly sweeping the stair
> I become aware
> Of a splendour that ties
> All the things of the earth
> To the things of the skies;

9

Here in my body the heavenly heat,
Here in my flesh the melodious beat
Of the planets that circle Divinity's feet,
As I go commonly sweeping the stair.

When one grasps this glorious inter-relation of all things in God's purpose of Life, it won't any longer seem worthy to put one's finger on an hour between eleven and twelve on Sunday morning and say, 'That's for worship,' or enough to set aside a few coins out of the middle of one's earnings and say, 'That's for God—I'll put it into the collection'. The whole of life must be dealt with as a piece. *Religion must make all the difference to everything, not some difference to a few things.* God wants ledgers kept and kindergarten classes taught. He wants soil tilled and foodstuffs sold across a counter. He wants honest councillors at the Town Hall and responsible politicians in Parliament. When we speak of men and women called 'to the ministry,' we know what we mean—but it isn't enough; we can't put a finger on to a particular piece of life and call it that—all life is a ministry. The Second Assembly of the World Council of Churches meeting at Evanston, found it necessary to underline this. 'The real battles of the Faith today,' ran its report to be read the world over, 'are being fought in factories, shops, offices and farms, in political parties and government agencies, in countless homes, in the press, radio and television, in the relationship of nations'.

It strikes one as odd, that at this late date, it was necessary to say it.

Kindle in our hearts a lasting love for Thy Great Self, O God; and for all good things Thou hast made. Amen.

Pietà

WASN'T it a mistake? That was my first thought. Would the millions crowding to New York for the World's Fair, be in the mood to look upon it? It seemed almost sacrilegious. But I was not consulted. Of all the sculptures I have studied in silence the world round, none has meant anything like as much to me as Michelangelo's 'Pietà'. And now for the first time, it was to leave the Vatican area, since the young sculptor himself placed it there in 1500. He was only twenty-four when he completed that lovely representation of Mary, the mother of our Lord, and the limp body of her Son. 'Sorrow in Stone' it has been called; and, though the sculptor lived to be almost ninety, I believe he created no other work of such flawless beauty.

The figure of Mary is that of a youthful, graceful mother. The beauty of her face as she looks down upon the crucified body of Him she has borne, in the purpose of God, to be the Saviour of men, suggests an agelessness. Suffused with deep feeling, one cannot look upon it, without being involved. Whatever violence the Crucifixion has shown in the past, the nail marks in hands and feet are barely discernible. The young Christ sleeps peacefully, the battle ended, the victory won over hate and man's last enemy Death, so soon to be vindicated in the open Tomb on Easter morning.

It is not surprising that the youthful creator of this conception of the deepest depths our human spirits can share, isolated himself from his companions as he worked upon it. Only as he knew exhaustion did he sleep, flinging himself down for an hour or two, fully dressed; and rising, pick up his hammer and chisel again. Two years passed; but there is a timelessness about it all.

Five feet nine inches in height, weighing twenty-seven

hundredweight; facts of this kind are the least to be remembered about 'Pietà'. Here is something so right, so graceful, so diffused with spiritual significance, that life for the beholder can never be quite the same again.

To begrudge those with deep, human needs like one's own, the privilege of looking upon it in the milling throngs of the World's Fair, is surely wrong. From the ends of the earth they will make their way. And colour, clime and condition will count for nothing.

> *'There is no God,' the foolish saith,*
> *But none, 'There is no sorrow.'*
> *And nature oft the cry of faith,*
> *In bitter need will borrow :*
> *Eyes which the preacher could not school,*
> *By wayside graves are raised,*
> *And lips say, 'God be pitiful',*
> *Who ne'er said, 'God be praised!'*

In these choice words Elizabeth Barrett Browning reminds me of a lasting fact. And I pray that the presence of Michelangelo's 'Pietà' has made the journey to New York worthwhile for someone.

Eternal God, I bless Thee for the countless ways in which Thy holy Love is shown—the grandeur and beauty of the world, the courageous voice of the prophet, the songs of the psalmist, the words of the gospel-writer. I bless thee for the sensitivity of the artist in colour and form. But far above all these, I bless Thee for the revelation of Thy heart in Jesus Christ. Amen.

Our Symbols

A SURPRISING experience befell me last night. I had been to dinner with friends in the city, and after pleasant talk over coffee, left for home. I started up the car under the starry sky, pulled out on to a steep private road serving several homes and headed for the main thoroughfare.

Suddenly, in the path of my headlights, I espied two huddled figures. Next moment, a lady and gentleman, looking up from the grassy verge, were explaining things.

'We were seeing friends off,' said he.

'As their car took on speed', added the wife, 'I flung out my arm to wave—and my wedding-ring flew off and is lost. We've looked and looked', added she wistfully.

'You need my torch,' I suggested, feeling in the pocket of the car.

Minutes later—and some distance off, re-searching all likely places—we found the ring.

'Oh, *thank* you,' ejaculated the wife, all but overcome; and hardly knowing how to receive it back, 'God bless you!'

A chance visitor from another planet might have counted it a lot of fuss over a little band of gold. Any number might be bought from any jeweller's. But, of course, it wasn't so simple—that little band of gold was a symbol. Without what it stood for, life for the loser would be insupportable.

A thin iron ring was given as a sign of bethrothal by the Romans, though the fifth century was on its way when the gold marriage-ring came into use, enjoying ecclesiastical sanction. Since then, it has gathered for us a very real significance. We live, as Hegel said, by 'materialized thinking'. To bring out the full meaning of things that touch us closely, we need our symbols; we can't do without them.

So the point is *not whether we shall have symbols or not, but which we will have, and what we will do with them.* A cross, a crucifix, lighted candles, and immediately we are involved in Christian controversy; but symbols are not limited to these. Without them, the pleasant, meaningful habit of shaking hands must be dropped from life, the kissing of one's child, the raising of one's hat, the saluting of the flag, the acceptance of the bread and wine at the service of communion. But again, we are back beyond daily events, to the things of our faith. Symbols have a habit of doing this. Thackeray tells us—though we seldom or never think of him as a religious man—what the crane on Corstorphine Hill, silhouetted, cross-like, against the evening sky, meant to him. Suddenly he exclaimed, 'Calvary!'

An ordinary chair at a retreat became for those who attended with Horton of Hampstead, the means of a similar quickening of spirit. At the opening, he explained, as chairman, how important it was that they should realize that it was not he, but their Lord and Master Who was really presiding. And suiting the action to the word, he thereupon stepped aside, vacating the chair throughout the remainder of the retreat.

'It sounds nothing,' said one who was there, 'but the effect was almost overwhelming.'

The symbol had truly served.

But we cannot by-pass Dr. Sangster's word of shock and warning. 'I went to a great meeting in the city of Gloucester,' said he. 'A large number of ministers were present on the platform. One of them, sitting in front of me, had a gold cross on his watch-chain. Imagine my horror to notice him during the speaker's address absent-mindedly use the corner of the cross to clean his finger-nails. I turned sick inside ... To such awful abuse can the most solemn symbol be turned!'

Eternal Father, in this quiet, before the clamant demands of the day break in, speak through common things to my needy heart. And make me aware of Thee. Amen.

Noughts and Crosses

MORNING by morning I walk a mile or so along a country road. At a junction there is a bus-stop. Skipping Saturdays and Sundays, three children join the school-bus there. Usually they stand with their bags in the sun; but this morning a sharp shower fell before I reached them. I found them instead in a little shelter, playing noughts-and-crosses. Whilst two crouched over a half-sheet from an exercise-book on the shelter bench, the third watched. So intent were they, that I thought I was going to miss my usual morning greeting.

We've all at some time played the fascinating old game—the paper ruled with a double-cross to make nine spaces. So simple is it that it can be played with a few minutes to spare at a bus-stop; so old that it reaches back into antiquity. Nobody knows where it was first played. But I was interested when in Maidstone, to step into All Saints'.

'It's a very old church,' whispered my friend, in whose home I was staying, as we paused a moment in the porch, 'mentioned in "Doomsday Book"—not this building as it is now, of course, but a church stood here as long ago as that.'

I had read how Pepys had visited Maidstone, and had written in his famous Diary: 'Up to the top of the steeple, had a noble view, and then down again!'

'Into All Saints', as the day ended,' was all I could write into mine, 'a moment's quiet—then out again.'

But I had time enough to seek out the verger and ask about a fascinating feature, the 'Noughts and Crosses'. Could he help me? Yes, he could. And carefully lifting a covering wooden seat, there, before my eyes, was the diagram identical to the one the children had drawn this morning in the bus-shelter, deeply scratched into a stone seat beneath.

' "Ovid's game", they called it,' explained the verger, 'origin of our Noughts and Crosses. Even the religious of old times needed some relaxation during a long sermon.'

Time, of course, moved slowly then, and sermons, we know from well-established sources, could be abnormally long. All Saints' pattern of noughts-and-crosses fascinated me. As I continued on, past the children in the bus-shelter this morning, G. K. Chesterton's striking words came back: 'All religions,' he said, 'are *either noughts or crosses.*'

And that is true! Jesus, our Lord, did not call men to nought; He called them to a cross. 'If any man will come after Me,' said He, 'let him deny himself, and take up his cross and follow Me' (Matt 16: 24). He knew the significance of what He was saying, and later, they knew, too. A cross is costly—far removed from the way in which we have smoothed, stylized it, jewelled it. Rammed into the solid earth, centre of the barbarous cruelty of crucifixion, it stood for a terrible reality. When Jesus faced the alternative of being put to silence or put to death. He knew what His choice had to be—a Cross. He could not go back on what He knew of the nature and message of God. He lived by it—and if it meant death, He had to die by it.

To such complete commitment He called men—and calls us *still!*

Everliving Lord, let Thy words echo in my heart this day, till my dedication is instant and complete. Multiply through me, the ministries of Thy love. Amen.

In the Waste-paper Basket

WHAT is your waste-paper basket worth to you? I don't mean to buy, but to use. One thing is certain, if you are a tidy person, a writer, or a parson, you can't function without it. I have a beauty. I didn't buy it: it was a gift from one of my twin sister's twin sons, clever with his hands.

Office space in London's West End, I am told, is now at a premium. At three pounds a square foot, plus rates, it is affecting the shape of waste-paper baskets. Some are being suspended from the ceiling, others have been replaced by long, slender, cylindrical dumps. In at least one instance known to me they have been replaced by a specially designed drawer for litter fitted into each desk. A good, old-fashioned waste-paper basket, it is suddenly realized, can take up to five pounds' worth of space each week.

Yet one can't get on in this busy, over-crowded life *without the continual selection and rejection one's waste-paper basket represents.*

It is attended with risks, of course. That little gem of music, MacDowell's 'To a Wild Rose', was found in manuscript at the bottom of a waste-paper basket. Its composer had thrown it away as worthless; yet what joy and inspiration it has since brought to countless thousands!

Kipling's 'Recessional' is another example. One morning it lay on the desk of the Editor of *The Times*. He was busy; he spared it a quick glance, then threw it into the waste-paper basket. Fortunately, moments later—on second thoughts—he fished it out again.

Over seventy years ago, Ernest Renan made a striking prophecy. 'I predict,' said he, 'that the twentieth century will spend a good deal of its time picking out of the waste-basket things which the nineteenth threw into it.' We are well into the twentieth century now; and it is time we began to think about this prophecy. Is it true? What are the things of value in danger of being lost, unless we look at them a second time?

First, I would put the *habit of family church-going*. It is easy to excuse our poorly filled churches today by saying that nobody attends unless he wants to; that in the nineteenth century it took more courage to stay away. But that isn't the final answer. 'People like my parents,' says J. B. Priestley, 'attended places of worship. Now I see that old phrase with a fresh eye. I also see how astonishing it is. Places of worship. *How much have we lost, we of the younger generations, by having no places of worship?* Perhaps this new world must remain desolate at heart until it achieves new places of worship.'

What he is saying is, 'Look again at what you have thrown away, and see if it is not worth picking out of the "waste-paper basket"?'

And there are many other precious things that we have valued little, of which the same might be said—*self-discipline, respect for superiors* including parents, *personal responsibility*. But the list grows long. In no case has the casting out of these timeless values brought us success or happiness. Rather the reverse. Life for many in our day has become like a great office, into which, crowding for space and attention, come too many things. The time has more than come for us to think again and see if we would not be wise to stoop humbly in sight of the God Who made us, and pick out of the 'waste-paper basket' some of these precious things.

O God, Thou hast fashioned us for a large purpose so that we cannot crowd our life into a little space. Help us to recognize the things of lasting worth. Amen.

He Noticed Things

WHEN news came up our green valley that Ian Graham had died, we all knew that we had lost not only a good farmer, but a good friend. We had worked and worshipped together. But our loss, of course, was nothing compared with that of Jeannie his wife.

Nearly a year has gone by, and when today I learned that Jeannie had had his grave beside the little country church 'done-up', I was curious to know what words she had chosen for his stone. Ian was not a man of words; to my knowledge, he never made a speech in his whole life. Anything she set there would have to be simple, if it was to suit Ian; but I was deeply touched to learn that the tribute chiselled there was no longer than three words: '*He noticed things*'.

Those words don't appear in Scripture in exactly that form, but the something God-like that they represent is there from end to end. And I can't think of a lovelier tribute. The relationship between Ian and his wife and family was something we all rejoiced in. The three youngsters, each in turn, counted on it—that strong, sane, down-to-earth joy in life, that forward-looking interest, that unwearying patience, that encouragement that showed itself chiefly in a look, an attitude. He noticed things. Whether the day went badly or well, there was strength in that fact.

'God,' says a modern preacher, 'is like that.' We sometimes think of Him as remote. But no; He notices things. Adds Rev. D. W. Cleverley-Ford, 'He notices the man in a tangle in some rudimentary prayer ... Or the woman unhappy at the seeming pointlessness of life, fingering thoughtfully that almost unused white confirmation prayer-book which once was given her. God notices her. And the man who has entered no church for years . . . God notices him.'

We do not find this as difficult to believe as we should have done, had Jesus not told us that supremely human-divine story of the lad who got away from home. When things turned out badly, and beaten out of his youthful pride, he turned homewards, most must have given up interest in him. 'But when he was yet a great way off, his Father saw him.' Day after day, his eyes, shaded from the light, that he might see clearer and further, had searched that road for the first stirring of the dust, the first sign of a figure. Out of his great love he knew how things might be; through all the years of growth and choice and error of his son, he had noticed things—and that power did not fail him now. God, said Jesus, is like that—you can't make a choice, or experience a change without His noticing—not only to chastise, to correct, but to encourage, and to rejoice in as a son (Luke 15: 11–32).

This is a great wonder to us ordinary people. We are not colourful characters—we don't run off in an impetuous moment to live under the bright lights of the far country —but we know the ups-and-downs of life, here and now; we suffer, we succeed, we fail, we dream.

Again and again we find Jesus demonstrating this. An old, bent woman, after years of suffering, entered the synagogue, and Luke tells us: '*Jesus noticed her* . . .' (Luke 13: 12, Moffatt). Exactly! 'As He passed along,' we read, 'He saw Levi' (Mark 2: 14, Moffatt). Day after day, he sat there at the receipt of custom, eating his heart out, his job growing always less satisfying; but only the Son of God noticed!

So I find myself pondering those three simple words Jeannie has chosen.

O Lord, bless all my dealings with others this day—that I may not fail them, nor Thee. Amen.

Window-cleaners

WHEN we built 'West Hills' we set our hearts on spacious windows—and now we rejoice in them. To the east they greet the new day, and give us a glimpse of a wooded inlet of the sea; to the west a valley girdled with trees gives way to heights. But when we come to window-cleaning we have problems, especially in that part where they are high off the ground.

For centuries, home-lovers had no such problems; the first window was little more than a narrow slit in the wall, uncomfortably called 'Wind's eye', from the Old Norse, 'vindauga'. In time, skins were stretched over it, and, later, tapestry. It was not until 1238, that King Henry III ordered a window of 'white glass' for the Queen's chamber at Winchester, 'that it may not be as windy as it used to be'. But it was rare, within the next three centuries, to find glass fixed in the openings of dwellings, even in castle walls.

Today, we set our window-cleaning against the joy of our wide panes of glass as a small price to pay; and Dr James Moffatt's words have significance for us when he describes his translation of the Scriptures, as 'simply a job of window-cleaning in literature'. We owe him a great debt; he has widened our view, and clarified it. Oddly, those who in 1611, gave us our Authorized Version thought of themselves as doing much the same sort of thing: 'Translation it is,' they said, in the language and limited conception of the day, 'that *openeth the window* to let in the light.'

A great deal has been learned since—manuscripts have been discovered, a closer study of the kind of language used by the sacred scribes has been made, together with a growing realization of the changing meaning of words in themselves. For these reasons, as Dr C. S. Lewis says: 'If we are to have translation at all, we must have periodical re-translation. There is no such thing as translating a book into another language once and for all.' *The task of window-cleaning must go on.*

So we welcome Dr James Moffatt's effort, followed by others—Monsignor Ronald Knox, with the New Testament in 1945, and the whole Bible ten years later; the scholars who in 1952 gave us the Revised Standard Version; Dr J. B. Phillips, who gave us the first of his books of the New Testament in 1947; and now, centuries after the Authorized Version, the company of scholars who have given us the New English Bible. Consideration of a handful of words makes it plain enough that we stand in constant need of this kind of help. Passages in the Authorized Version, for all their long association and majestic beauty, no longer in some cases, say the things originally intended. The same is true of individual words: 'prevent' is used not in the modern sense, 'to hinder', but in the old sense, 'to precede'—so the Psalmist prays, 'O God . . . let Thy tender mercies speedily prevent us' (Psa 79: 8; 'cunning' is used for skill (as in Psa 137: 5); 'Comfort' (as in Psa 23: 4) has lost a lot of its strength, till it has become associated with armchair ease, smooth pillows and soothing words; 'conversation' (as used in Psa 50: 23) was originally a matter of general conduct rather than speech; and there is the famous word 'charity', so demeaned by patronage that it no longer carries the glory of love first intended (as in I Cor 13). And now, the word 'love' has become so sentimentalized and nauseatingly commercialized, that soon, it seems, we must look for another. So the work goes on.

Blessings on all window-cleaners!

O Lord, I rejoice in every means by which Thy good will becomes known. Amen.

No U Turn

IT doesn't surprise me that a country driver bringing his car to the city often finds himself in a fix. Traffic signs that are meant to help multiply daily. I found myself today in a familiar city street; but since I was last there it has acquired a sign: 'No U Turn'.

If it has been invented earlier, our nursery-books would have been the poorer—we should never have heard of Dick Whittington. With his staff and his bundle, we met him sitting dejected on his milestone, the towers and spires of the great city rising from the distant landscape. The city had been cruel to him, and he was ready to turn his back on its fascinating aspects, its greatness and challenge. Then the sound of Bow Bells came to him, sweet and clear on the morning air, ' *Turn again, turn again, turn again*, Whittington, Lord Mayor of London!' At that, our loved story-book said, young Dick got up, turned resolutely about, and went back to find honour and fame. A 'No U Turn' set in a hedge, or hammered on a tree-trunk, and there would have been no story.

The same may be said of that fiery, determined little Jew hurrying down the Damascus Road. We know him as Paul—but a 'No U Turn' anywhere there on that road would have meant that we should never have known him at all! That would have been loss enough for us; but a tragedy to the Church of Christ in the world. But there was no such sign. So the story has its dynamic, caught by the modern-day poet in half-a-dozen lines:

> *A desert way,*
> *A burning sun,*
> *And—Saul.*

A sudden light,
A heavenly voice
And—Paul.

Those of us who follow on, have never been able to surpass that moment—or dispense with it. It is all very well to receive us gently into the Church, with infant baptism; but the time always comes, when of age, we must pass down our own Damascus Road. We cannot easily, unknowingly slip into the Kingdom; though we have been brought up in love to worship and serve, the time comes when we must confront the Christ. For some, it may be a matter of continuing on the way our feet are set; but for very many more it is a matter of 'Turn again!' And if there were a 'No U Turn' there, what should we do? The Scriptural word is: 'Repent . . . and turn again, that your sins may be blotted out' (Acts 3: 19, R.S.V.).

The Church calls this experience 'conversion', though some of us, it seems, are a little shy about using it. The word comes from the Latin 'convertere', 'to cause to turn', 'to turn about', 'to turn back'. One is surprised that John Wesley, who witnessed so many sudden conversions, and rejoiced in their reality, should have written, 'It is a term indeed, which I rarely use, because it rarely occurs in the New Testament'.

It is not, of course, *always* a sudden thing. To this mistake some add that of thinking that the 'about turn' must come to all alike. This we know from Paul's experience and ten thousand others since is not so. A further mistake is to ignore the life-long learning that follows.

Thank God, no modern sign blocks our spiritual way!

Confronted, forgiven, enlightened, let me face this new day, O Lord. Let none of yesterday's mistakes remain to spoil today's opportunities. For Christ's sake. Amen.

Imagine It!

IF you had told me as I sat in Synod on Monday that before the end of the week I would be battling across the Atlantic in a little twenty-three-foot boat, I wouldn't have believed you—yet this has happened.

I'd better, perhaps, be a bit more explicit. The truth is, I wakened on Tuesday morning with a streaming dose of 'flu, every joint aching. The first thing was to get a message to Synod; the next—between inhalations and lemon drinks —to seek fresh company. I was lucky enough to fall in with Ann Davison, the first woman to cross the Atlantic alone in a tiny craft, the *Felicity Ann*. Through the good offices of her publisher, Peter Davies, she agreed to take me with her.

I don't mind admitting there were times in the next days and nights, when I wondered if we'd make it. Plymouth Sound behind, we were to be cold, lonely and frightened a dozen times before we got to Douarenez, to Vigo and Gibraltar. And after that, things got worse—out beyond Casablanca, pushing into mountainous seas—too sick at times to even trim the sails properly, barnacles and assorted marine growths of other kinds, reducing the *F.A.*'s six knots. Fuel ran low, fresh water threatened to give out, and plain human strength likewise. During the thousands of exposed miles to Antigua, calms came to be as dangerous in their way as squalls. It was touch-and-go. I can't think I was ever more thankful for anything than to reach New York, Pier 9, *still alive!*

There are such times when imagination is a painful gift, ministering to fear; but, by and large, it is a power indispensable to full life. How awful to be shut in with the dull miseries of 'flu, with no such means of escape! For imagination is not just a power valued by children, story-tellers,

25

and dramatists. It is that—and more. Sympathy, under-standing and tolerance depend on it. Every piece of compassionate service, every great undertaking, has first to be 'imaged in the mind'. It is the way of endless enrichment. 'Thou wilt keep him in perfect peace,' says Scripture, 'whose mind (R.V. *marg:* imagination) is stayed on Thee' (Isa. 26: 3).

Imagination allows us to live fully—to live excitingly, to live in the past, consorting with heroes and heroines, to reconstruct modern adventure, Bible stories, and sagas. 'The human mind,' Professor Macneile Dixon reminds us, 'is not, as philosophers would have us think, a debating hall, but a picture-gallery. Imagination rules all our lives.'

Above all, it is the power by which we know how life looks to the other fellow. It was in this sense that Ann Davison—when still learning seamanship—pondered boat-builder Jake's unexpected remark. They shared a small yard, unpretentious, half-hidden, save to the plover, curlew, and wild duck, up a tidal creek in the south of England. 'The owner, Jake'—to fall back on Ann's telling of it—'was tall, dark and bearded, stern and withdrawn, given to sudden flashes of disarming affability. He could build a boat, renovate a wreck, a radio, or an engine with equal facility and consummate skill. He wrote articles for the technical press, and novels on the side.' And that was not all. 'He once,' said Ann, 'remarked after a long silence and *a propos* of nothing at all, "You talk about imagination, but no one has anything on the Lord".'

Exactly! Turn up the Old and New Testaments, and read of His dealings with men and women like you and me.

O Lord, show me how to use well my every faculty; for Thy Name's sake. Amen.

Stir-up Sunday

Of all the Feasts and Festivals of the Christian Year few of us know Stir-up Sunday, which is a pity. In old cookery-books we may happen on a recipe for a delicious confection, 'Stir-up Sunday cake'; but the whole is much more than that.

This Sunday before Advent gets its name from the opening words of the Collect for the day: 'Stir up, we beseech Thee, O Lord, the wills of Thy faithful people; that they, plenteously bringing forth the fruit of good works, may of Thee be plenteously rewarded; through Jesus Christ our Lord. Amen.'

Men and women have needed stirring up from the beginning of time. In *a national sense* it has always been easy to slip into apathy, casualness, indolence, till even the most august and splendid allegiances touch us not at all. It was a situation of this kind that moved Isaiah the prophet to cry: 'There is none that calleth upon Thy name, that stirreth up himself to take hold of Thee' (Isa. 64: 7). Here is a baffling and frustrating frame of mind, a general attitude of superficial comfort and carelessness.

But the challenge of Stir-up Sunday comes to us, too, with *a personal connotation*. And in this, we are linked one by one, with fellow-Christians before us. To young Timothy, Paul wrote in that thrilling first century: 'Stir up the gift of God which is in thee' (II Tim. 1: 6). So there was need for this challenge even then! It had bearing in the first case, no doubt, on the special gift of the Spirit granted him at ordination; but it has lasting significance for those of us in the Christian circle beyond the ordained ministry.

When the great moments pass, it is all too easy to fall into lethargy, to bother less and less about the basic truths that stirred us once, to offer service of a less thorough-going kind.

John Buchan wrote of his father—minister of the Church of Scotland—in admiration, for the lasting way in which he recognized this. 'He believed profoundly in the fact of "conversion",' said he, 'the turning of the face to a new course. But the first step having been taken, he would insist upon the arduousness of the pilgrimage, as well as upon its moments of high vision . . . He had no love for those who took their ease in Zion!'

Nor has anyone else, much less the Christ Who calls us. The challenge that comes to us each, is to *stir up* the gift of God which is in us.

Reporting on the character of world-wide Christian service and opportunity today, the World Council of Churches underlines for each of us this very point; in Section III of one of its publications, these words appear: 'In all these fields, the real dangers are complacency, lack of imagination, and the dull sense of hopelessness that settles upon those of little faith.' How can it be otherwise, unless one by one, *we stir up* the gift of God? To take pride in the world-wide nature of the Church, and falter in witness as an indivdual; to rejoice in the continuing revelation of God's truth to scholars and saints, and not live in what is granted to oneself, is a double pity. Death begins where liveliness ceases. Stir-up Sunday comes but once a year; but I see no reason why I might not celebrate it much more often. Do you? Surely our Lord and Master intends goodness to be adventurous, truth to be exciting, service to be satisfying, humility winsome!

Forgive me, O God, where I fail to show forth in my life standards I expect of others. Amen.

In the Same Country

IT is a shock to Christians the world over to have barbed-wire outside Bethlehem, marking the boundary between Israel at enmity with Jordan.

But then there was nothing 'pretty-pretty' about that first Christmas—taxes were as unpleasant then as now; eighty dusty miles of travel an exhausting business, specially for a young woman 'near her time'; an inn-door slammed-to, doubly dispiriting.

In his *Naught For Your Comfort*, Trevor Huddlestone describes a cold December night in Sophiatown on the fringe of Johannesburg, where families sheltered in shabby, flimsy shacks. That night a husband returned from work to find his shanty dismantled by the authorities, and his wife in labour in front of a brazier. Their baby was born under the canopy of the winter stars. Says Huddleston, 'In that dejected scene in Edith Street, the picture of Bethlehem came to life.'

When in the fullness of Time, God sent forth His Son, 'made of a woman . . . to redeem', there was 'no room for them in the inn'. Luke, the physician-scribe, filled in the outlines with sympathy. But its background was stark; the decree from Caesar Augustus, Emperor of Rome, was heartless and removed from the personal concerns of common people, his dominion extending beyond lands of the Mediterranean, over seas eastward to Asia. What he ordered was done; wherever his legions marched, men were obliged to make way.

It was a world wherein little ones, newly-born, could claim no public consideration. And in a very little time, Herod would be clashing in upon the scene with low cunning and cruelty, setting young couples like Mary and Joseph wailing

29

for their murdered little ones. With its evil, and fear of those in high places, its instability in local administration, its apathy, rooted selfishness and sorrow widespread, it was a dark world.

But when Luke has sketched it in—the evil nature of things—as he so clearly can, he reminds us of *one fact more*. And in a world like our own, that has become dark for many, it is a fact to remember: 'There were,' he says, 'in the same country shepherds abiding in the field, keeping watch over their flock by night' (Luke 2: 8). Oh, yes, the evil was real enough; it was a dark time of Roman might, of heartless domination; the rich alone able to secure without question the comfort of the open inn-door, and withal to carouse within.

'But in the same country there were sheperds.' Luke wants us never to overlook that surprising fact. It is so easy to take account of the powerful, the evil, the blatant, and forget the shepherds. They represent for all time the ordinary, honest-to-goodness people in every situation. This is the encouraging fact revealed in Bethlehem and in history since—the note struck at an ecumenical conference by Rev. Alan Brash, General Secretary of the National Council of Churches, on this side of the world: 'It is wrong,' said he, 'to think of Moscow as unconditionally Red evil. It is not. The Orthodox Church is now much stronger than in 1917 —twenty-thousand Christian communities meet for worship in Russia.'

God still has His shepherds ready to serve Him!

Almighty God, my Father, Thou hast Thy faithful men and women everywhere—many serving where no one notices, who ask no reward save the joy of doing Thy will on earth. Number me amongst them, this day, I pray Thee. Amen.

God's Greatest Thought

No wonder the inner secret of Christmas escapes many of us—we're so noisy. We seem incapable of thinking of a thing, or working at a thing, except against a background of noise—as though there were something indecent about silence. Nietzsche seldom said anything that I want to treasure in my heart, but I love the way he said: 'Thoughts that come on tip-toe move the world'—that is, thoughts that come silently.

Certainly that is true of *God's Greatest Thought*—which became audible in the Incarnation. 'Why,' asks Dr C. F. Hunter, the theologian, 'was Jesus Christ described as "the Word" or "Logos"?' And as tellingly, he answers that question. 'A thought is a spiritual thing, invisible and inaudible; a sound is a material thing, a movement of air; but a word is a combination of the two, a thought become audible, so that it is spiritual and material at the same time. A word is a thought embodied in a material form. Jesus Christ was the Word of God, that is, the mind and will and love of God uttered forth in a material form by His becoming flesh. He was God's expression of Himself in a human life.'

And how silently that Thought comes still—on tip-toe, as it were, to move the world!

> *How silently, how silently*
> *The wondrous gift is given!*
> *So God imparts to human hearts*
> *The blessings of His heaven.*
> *No ear may hear His coming;*
> *But in this world of sin,*
> *Where meek souls will receive Him, still*
> *The dear Christ enters in.*

In this age of noise, it surprises us. We are so enamoured of the pneumatic drill, the factory whistle, the stamp of mighty news-presses, the screech of brakes, the stridency of telephone bells, that we forget how often God works His will this way. 'Man's work is accompanied by so much noise; if he desires a silver cup for sacraments, there must go to its fashioning,' Mary Webb reminds us, 'the sound of hammering, the scratch of a chisel, the roar of a furnace; but when the innumerable chalices of the privet are made ready for the hawk-moth's first taste of honey, there is no stir at all. The aisle and transepts of our temples rise with clamour of voice and commotion of labour . . . but the aisles of pines down a mountain side, the transept of beeches in a valley rise as softly as a thought.'

But a thought does not remain a thought—it becomes that which coming, as it were, on tip-toe, moves the world. Who remembers now those who noisily caroused in an over-crowded inn in Bethlehem, when God's Thought was born, clothed in flesh to become His Word? *But He goes on moving this world!* Who cares that the narrow ways of an ancient city echoed with the noisy cry, 'Crucify Him! Crucify Him!'? The world-moving fact today is an empty Tomb in a Garden nearby, vacated silently whilst men and women slept, exhausted. *So He goes on moving this world!*

With good reason, Scripture urges us—and never more fittingly than at this season—'Be silent to the Lord, and wait patiently for Him', or as translated nearer our own time, 'Be silent to God, and let Him mould thee.'

I bless Thee, O Lord, for Christ's coming, His growth, and glorious ministry here. Let my life reflect something of His spirit. Amen.

Taking Levels

SINCE student days I have loved Christchurch, New Zealand. To an impressionable young adult, she was beautiful even then—and knew it—the city of the plains, 'each of her streets,' as the poet said, 'closed with shining Alps, like heaven at the end of long plain lives.' Her leisurely river, overhung with graceful willows, added coolness and charm, banks grassed to the water's edge. Her beautiful tree-filled squares—bearing the names of English martyrs, Latimer, Ridley, Cranmer—introduced a strong sense of history, and spiritual indebtedness. But even more striking, then as now, was her Cathedral with tall spire, set in the square. He would be dull indeed, who missed its significance.

To step inside is to have one's eyes fall upon an inscription which reads: *On the floor below this wall is the bench mark, twenty feet above mean sea-level at Lyttelton, from which all other levels in Christchurch are calculated.*

So the surveyor and builder, set to raise a block of offices in the city, or a school, hospital, or aerodrome in the suburbs, must take his levels from within the Cathedral. What a significant thing! To step inside the Cathedral is to stumble upon a parable—things sacred are seen to affect things secular; and what is found established in the House of God to govern men and women in their business and home life. Thus in the holy place, two worlds meet, and are known to be interdependent.

It doesn't take long to discover that there are many things in this life which refuse to work out, till they take their 'levels' from the place of the spirit. Without that, human relationships become a maze. 'Plagued, and chastened every morning,' as the Psalmist describes himself, he adds as the secret of the experience, 'It was too painful for me,

33

until I went into the sanctuary of God' (Psa. 73: 14–17). On another occasion it is a distressing letter that comes to one immersed in human affairs. 'And Hezekiah,' we read, 'received the letter of the hand of the messenger, and read it.' What next? 'Hezekiah went up into the house of the Lord, and spread it out before the Lord' (II Kings 19: 14). He was taking his 'levels'. From there he could move out into life. Happy is the modern man who is as sure where the 'levels' are! Peter Marshall, faithful young chaplain, expresses this essential in his prayer at the opening of Senate: 'Help us to stand for something, that we may not fall for everything.' Only in the presence of God, in the place of worship and prayer, can we be sure of the 'levels' by which life can be governed. Our own late King, George the Sixth, discovered that. The night before his Coronation, the Dean of Westminster received a telephone call.

'I want to come to the Abbey tonight.'

'Certainly, sir,' came the reply, 'I will be there to receive you.'

'No, don't do that,' the King answered, 'I want you to see that the postern door is left open. I wish to come into the Abbey and I wish to be alone.'

And that night the man, who on the morrow would be immersed in pomp and circumstance, and whom from that moment all the world would involve in leadership, wanted to be sure of his 'levels'.

This, for the highest and the least of us, is the ministry of the House of God—in public worship, and in private devotion.

Almighty God, I marvel that men have ceaselessly sought Thee. Beside many altars they have made their prayers, and set the level of their lives. I bless Thee for Jesus Christ, against Whom all things human and divine are measured. Amen.

Come—Gently—On

UNDER the mantle of the prince, and the thread-bare jacket of the prodigal, is the knowledge that there is no dodging Death. Paul called it 'the Last Enemy'. Science can now prolong our days on this earth, but so far there is no hope that 'the Last Enemy' can be by-passed. Paul Tillich says that fear of Death is our basic anxiety. I wonder is that so? Some grow morbid about it; but is there need to do that?

Said Ellen Terry, calmly and clearly, as she prepared her Will, in readiness for that moment:

> *No funeral gloom my dears when*
> *I am gone,*
> *Corpse-gazing, tears, black*
> *raiment, grave-yard grimness,*
> *Think of me as withdrawn into the*
> *dimness,*
> *Yours still, you mine. Remember*
> *all the best*
> *Of our past moments, and forget*
> *the rest,*
> *And so, to where I wait, come—*
> *gently—on!*

This is the Christian approach to Death. When Christ Himself drew near to the end of His earthly life, He prepared Himself, and those He loved, *not for extinction, but for a larger experience*. He shed no tears of farewell. And His gallant confidence echoed in the hearts of all who came into living relationship with Him: 'Be of good cheer, I have overcome the world!' 'I am the Resurrection and the Life!' 'Because 1 live, ye shall live also!' Is it not the most wonderful, natural, logical thing that the chapter in which

35

those words of His appear—14th of John—should be treasured above most by Christian men and women? 'Let not your heart be troubled,' it begins, 'ye believe in God, believe also in Me,' or as the New English Bible puts these words of quiet assurance: 'Set your troubled hearts at rest. Trust in God always; trust also in Me. There are many dwelling-places in My Father's house; if it were not so I should have told you; for I am going there on purpose to prepare a place for you.' This is something more than sweet solace for private grief—though it is that. It is an essential of our Christian faith—confirmed by Christ Himself in His resurrection, underlined in Scripture, recited in Creeds, and sung in ten thousand hymns. And nowhere is its glorious reality better shown than in the dedication of Dr A. J. Gossip's book—one of many at arms-length from where I write these words, and often open in my hands, to the strengthening of my faith—'To my wife, now a long time in the Father's House'; and that of one written by Pandit Nehru, and dedicated to his wife: 'To Kamala who is no more.' Such a world of difference—the difference between that which supports and quickens Christian hearts, and that of a faith that has no Risen Lord to say: 'Because I live, ye shall live also.' 'In My Father's House there are many dwelling-places ... I go to prepare a place for you.'

When the Way here finishes, Christ says to us one by one, *never fear;* the Door *will be opened to you from the Other Side!*

O Lord, Thou hast given me a life which this world cannot contain. Lead me continually into Thy great and holy purpose. Amen.

With Dry Eyes

A WORD here and there becomes out-of-date, like a hat, a coat, a car. I am always coming upon one marked 'obs'—obsolete.

But the word 'compassion' carries no such mark, and I can't think that it ever will. My dictionary defines it as, 'pity inclining one to spare or help.' I like the way it is linked to action. The first time I remember it being used in conversation was in what we now call 'the depression years'. I was a young social-worker in our largest city.

'*When Jesus was moved with compassion, He always did something,*' was a sentence used by a staff-member, with her sleeves rolled up. And it is something I've never forgotten.

Two hundred years or so before He moved among men and women, Cato, the Roman, gave advice to anyone who would farm his land to profit: 'Look over the livestock and hold a sale. Sell your oil, if the price is satisfactory, and sell the surplus of your wine and grain. Sell out-worn oxen, blemished cattle, blemished sheep, wool, hides, an old wagon, old tools'—so far so good, but when it goes on without drawing fresh breath to add—'an old slave, a sickly slave, and whatever else is superfluous,' we know it for a heartless piece of advice.

People who mattered to no one else mattered to Jesus. Again and again that moving, helpful word 'compassion' must be used in the record of His dealings. To leaf through the Gospels, is to hear of the poor, wretched leper. 'And Jesus, moved with compassion, put forth His hand, and touched him, and saith unto him, I will; be thou clean' (Mark 1: 41). His action was a very surprising one in those days—not only was He concerned for the unhappy leper—He touched him. And healing came. That was His personal

37

reaction. And to this day, no social agency, committee, or organization—however efficient—can quite take the place of personal concern. It is an essential part of compassion. A few pages further on into Mark's gospel, we read of the demented man among the tombs. Jesus was moved by his unhappy lot—and 'did something'. Restored, the man would have followed Jesus and His disciples, but His word to him was: 'Go home to thy friends, and tell them how ... the Lord hath had compassion on thee' (Mark 5: 19). A few pages on (Luke 7: 13) we come upon the record of the widow of Nain. She had but one son—and he died. Widows' sons died often enough and no one cared—but not in this case. Jesus chanced to meet the bier and its sorrowful procession. We are not told anything of the widow's social or religious standing, only of her grief. 'And when the Lord saw her, He had compassion on her, and said unto her, Weep not. And He came and touched the bier.' It is true: words were never enough—'when Jesus was moved with compassion, He always did something.'

And He urged the same sense of practical responsibility on those who listened to His words, as well as on those who witnessed His compassionate works. His story of The Good Samaritan turns on this very word. As the stranger, a Samaritan—much as we might say today, a Negro or a Communist—journeyed, he came upon need, a man badly beaten-up. 'And when he saw him, he had compassion on him'—but that we know by now, won't be all—'and went to him, and bound up his wounds ...' (Luke 10: 33–35).

So the challenge of compassion passes from our Lord to those of us who would follow in His way. It is not enough to be *moved by compassion;* we must act upon it.

It is this that Dr Frank C. Laubach, our dynamic modern-day Christian, means when he says: 'Lord, forgive us for looking at the world with dry eyes—and empty hands.'

Guests of God

I was taken out to dinner one evening this week to a popular city restaurant. I had never been there to a meal before. And in addition to a good meal, I found there something I have never seen in any public restaurant before—three Graces printed below the menu. One was headed 'Protestant', the second, 'Jewish', and the third 'Roman Catholic'.

The first ran: 'Bless, O Lord, this food to our use, and us to Thy service, and make us mindful of the needs of others, in Jesus' Name. Amen.' A good Grace, and familar to some of us.

The second ran: 'Lift up your hands towards the sanctuary and bless the Lord. Blessed art Thou, O Lord, our God, King of the universe Who bringest forth bread from the earth.'

The third read: 'Bless us, O Lord, and bless Thy gifts which we are about to receive from Thy bounty, through Christ our Lord. Amen.'

Young and old, city and country people were there, and a bus-load of tourists from afar, white, brown and black. But with all our differences, we shared our common need ot food. I found myself wondering how many used the three forms of Grace provided.

Grace before Meat is a simple act that some have dropped from life, which seems a great pity. Surely there was never a time when it was more relevant than now. Two-thirds of our fellow men, women and little children the world round never come to a table as satisfyingly served as that to which I drew up my chair on Tuesday evening. Many lie down in abject hunger. Donald K. Faris, of the United Nations Technical Assistance Administration, is right: 'If a man is hungry it does not matter where he comes from or what his background is—he is still *an indelicate and probably dangerous individual.* Under-nourishment calls forth the most basic urge in man—the urge for survival. It is this which has made hunger one of the most fundamental and explosive forces in history, and in the world today.'

Whilst we have a hungry world, we cannot have a world happy with its lot; and whilst that is so, we cannot hope for a world at peace.

Wonderful things are being done today by the U.N. Food and Agricultural Organization, by Inter-Church Aid and other organized groups—not only to feed the hungry, but to provide seeds, skills, fertilizers, tractors, etc., to make possible a more hopeful future for those in need.

It is a social pleasure to be taken occasionally to eat out; but it is even greater cause for thanksgiving, that three times a day our own table is satisfyingly spread. It is increasingly important in this kind of world in which we live, that we should acknowledge—as individuals and as a family—*how blessed we are, and how dependent.* Despite all our modern technology, for 'many-tasting food', we are 'Guests of God'. From Him comes that which we need. In the year 1565— just over four-hundred years ago, divided from us by the reigns of the First and Second Queen Elizabeth—one wrote this 'Grace before Meate':

> *God blesse our meate*
> *God blesse our waies*
> *God give us grace*
> *Our Lord to please.*
> *Lorde long p' serve in peace and health*
> *Our gracious queene Elizabeth.*

These are different days—but our blessings continue, and our dependency!

In the enjoyment of Thy good gifts, let us be unselfish and ever grateful. Amen.

In Gratitude

NIGHT after night just now, the air is chill, the stars above fresh and clear. I have had to be late several times this week. The light in the window has seemed specially welcoming as I've come up the hill.

Half-an-hour later, as I've snuggled into bed it's been easy to give thanks for Edmund Blanket; I nearly called him 'Saint' Edmund, but perhaps that is going a little too far.

When in Bristol, I was astonished to find how little any of my friends could tell me about him. One of them—after a jogging of memory—did recall the cautious historical note in St Stephen's Church, by way of description: 'Probably the effigies of Edmund Blanket, born in 1300, died 1380 . . . and his second wife Margaret, buried in a chantry in the Lady Chapel of the previous church on this site. In 1362, he was M.P. for Bristol. A woollen weaver by trade . . . the first to set up looms in England after the cloth-weaving revival . . . by tradition the inventor of an article of bedding, which still bears his name.'

It is through this last-mentioned gift that he touches my life most closely, and moves me to gratitude. What would one do on fresh, crisp nights like this, without Edmund Blanket? Many a one for less, has been canonized. Blessings on his memory!

Too many to whom we owe a lasting debt for the things of everyday, are allowed to slip into forgetfulness. With our faulty sense of proportion, we often raise public monuments to men who do much less for us. In many a case, even the *name* of our benefactor is allowed to slip from remembrance. In a speech in Dundee, Marconi referred to a 'Mr Anonymous' who stood by him at an important time in his career

—a Dundee worker in the same area of investigation, forty years earlier. 'Without that man of genius,' said Marconi, in acknowledging an honour to himself, 'my work would have been impossible.' But his name—no one knows his name! And how often if has been so. Paul speaks of fellow-workers 'as unknown, and yet well known' (II Cor. 6: 9). In his 'History of the English Speaking Peoples', Sir Winston Churchill refers to 'unknown and unremembered men.'

There are many. But as long as I live, ready for rest at the day's end, I'm going to keep the grateful memory of Edmund Blanket alive!

I cannot do as much for many another to whom I am indebted—the easterner, unknown, to whom I owe the shape of my bed; the originator of the cotton sheets that come between me and my good blankets; the silk-merchant to whom I am indebted for the covering of my eider-down; the hunter of the Arctic who discovered how warm and snug the breast-feathers of a duck can be; the brave who pioneered my moccasins; the Mohammedan to whom I owe the name of my night wear—'pyjamas', described as 'a suit of loose trousers and jacket'.

But there is no end to this call for gratitude. When I rise from sleep, to begin a new day, I am protected from malaria by the discovery of a Frenchman, Pasteur, and a German, Koch; from typhoid by the help of a Russian, Metchnikoff; from tetanus, by a Japanese, Kitasate; from small-pox, by an Englishman, Jenner.

Every hour—asleep or awake—I am surrounded by the gifts of men who never thought in terms of profit, of country, colour, or acclaim, who served no lesser loyalty than the welfare of mankind.

In my daily life, O Lord, I rejoice that no line can rightly be drawn between gifts sacred and gifts secular—all come from Thee, using men and women. Amen.

Such Hospitality

On my travels I came to a lovely home in the south. I had been hindered, and the hour was late; but it made no difference—the warm light of the hall that enveloped me when the door was opened to my knock was no more real than the loving consideration that wrapped me round during the whole of my visit. The table was set, though the children had had their meal and were in comfortable positions before the fire. After I had eaten, we shared a game of dominoes till bedtime.

Next morning I was let into a secret.

'Ruth,' said my hostess, 'is a funny wee dear. Every night when she says her prayers, she tells God the things that have happened during the day. Last night, whilst you sat at the fireside, I slipped upstairs to see them safely tucked in, and I overheard her: "Oh, yes, and there's another thing: we've got Sister Rita Snowden staying with us. We're allowed to call her 'Sister Rita'—it's quite all right; but her real name is 'Rita F. Snowden'—it's on her books. You can see it"!'

Delightful! In that instant, I knew that the hospitality of that lovely home was not alone of earth, but something which concerned our Father in Heaven as well. Nor was I surprised at that. There is a great deal in the New Testament about hospitality. Our Lord, when grown to adult-hood, had no home of His own to which He could invite folk; but without doubt, He had a hospitable soul, and found numerous ways in which to show hospitality. On one occasion, He was host to five thousand, gathered out-of-doors on the grass in little companies, picnic-fashion; at the end of His life—with the shadow of betrayal and death over Him—He was Master of a Last Supper with His disciples; and after the Crucifixion, and Resurrection, unchanged in this grace, we find Him greeting dispirited fishermen in the early grey of morning on the seashore with 'a little fire, and fish laid thereon'.

One of the loveliest echoes of the Lord's loving consideration is in Peter's injunction to fellow-Christians in the early Church—preserved for us in his Epistle: 'Be hospitable to each other and never grudge it' (I Peter 4: 9, Moffatt). Many Christians were on the road in those troublous times, apostles, teachers, refugees, hounded from place to place for the Faith. Lodging places were notoriously costly, dirty and immoral. It must have been wonderful for a way-faring Christian to find an open door, and to be received into a Christian circle. Peter knew something of that grace; so did Paul. He wrote: 'Serve the Lord; let your hope be a joy to you; be steadfast in trouble, attend to prayer, contribute to needy saints, make a practice of hospitality' (Rom. 12: 11–13, Moffatt).

So hospitality is something—as little Ruth supposes—that concerns God our Father, as do all out-reaching ministries of the human spirit. And today, more than most times, opportunities come to us to serve in this way—students from distant parts of the world, along with many of our own with white faces, are in every great city where educational facilities exist; nurses provided with hostel accommodation, are ever grateful to be received at a family fire-side; shy folk, lonely folk, anxious folk, flat dwellers, aged, and bereft are about us continually. To those who receive at our hands such hospitality, it is a rich gift; to those of us who can offer it, it is a duty and a privilege. From the start, Christians have understood that *religion must be expressed in the open door, the open hand, the open heart.*

O Lord, may my door be open wide to need; and shut tight to pride and strife. Amen.

There Never Was a Time . . .

GROWING-UP is far from being *all* fun. Not only do our present-day youngsters find themselves maturing early, but they are set to live in an unstable society—this makes things doubly difficult. Those of us who look on from the standpoint of years—parents, teachers, friends, critics, self-styled psychologists—need some patience.

It is so easy to damn the present generation as 'the worst ever'—each in its turn has been that. 'Where it hath ever been held that blushing in measure, modestie, and silence hath been commendable tokens in young yeares,' says one, 'nowe is it a shame to be ashamed.' But that wasn't headlined in this morning's paper—though only its spelling gives it away. Gervase Babington wrote that in the sixteenth century!

All too often conversation these days finds room for this sort of comment: 'Young folk are too blasé; they get too much done for them: their sports even are organized and drilled: and as a result, all the fine juice of the old enthusiasm of their fathers and grandfathers has been squeezed out oɪ them.' But Wilkie Collins said that first in 1860!

We ought to see that it's a pity to be too sweeping. When I hear one begin: 'There never was a time . . .' I know what will follow. But despite faults, youth is never *all* bad. I know as much as most of beatniks, of dirty, bearded, languid habitués in little dark coffee-bars—but their proportion in the community is small. I shudder at sight and sound of tough, leather-jerkined youths on motor-bikes, bearing down on corners, with their girls on pillions—but how many are there?

Some, it is true, get into the hands of the law; but by far the greater number of our youth get on with their schooling, engage in sport, go to work, and share in the laughter and wholesome responsibility of home-life. Of course, we never hear much of these—their names never get into the paper.

Our much-maligned youth must be measured against its parents, teachers, brothers, sisters, aunts, uncles, friends; and the kind of world we have. Many are required to *live in crowds*, at school and work, before they have learned *to live with themselves*. Small wonder that some fall prey to the strongest character they meet—though not necessarily the most morally or mentally mature.

Now and again, someone like sixteen-year-old Heather Marshall, speaking in a contest organized by the Rotary Club of Woking, gives us some idea of how things look to youth. And her words surprise us, when she describes the youth she knows, as 'sick of a surfeit of time and money, sick from lack of discipline, sick from excess of speed'. The materialistic standards of our day, she says, hold insufficient challenge for youth. 'Everything is laid on'.

The greater wonder, perhaps, is that so many manage to overcome these difficulties, and do things of lasting worth. Vacation-time now means for scores of teenagers, service for needy folk, old and the hungry, work-camps set on clearing derelict districts, laying out children's playgrounds, erecting fences on mission properties, and countless other enterprises. Youthful Mr Christopher Chataway, speaking lately at the London Federation of Boys' Clubs, struck the right note: 'In the energy and idealism of young people—much of it now bottled up or running to waste, there is a national source of power,' he said.

Grant Thy patience and wisdom, O God our Father, to all who have to do with youth, that together we may rejoice in strength, eagerness, and laughter. Amen.

My Hat!

I WENT to church today in my new hat—trying not to think of it, which was difficult. I suppose a woman's head has always counted less than her heart, in a place of worship; but till comparatively recent years, a woman without a hat in church would have been as conspicuous as Lady Godiva without her garments in the street.

Last year, according to statistics just to hand, British women spent a record £24,140,000 on hats—a million and a half more than any previous peak year. A reasonable proportion of these, it may well be supposed, found their way to worship.

Some may have been acquired because of the relentless on-going of fashion; others, at the inspiration of Nature—a stirring among living things, new leaves, blossoms breaking forth, and who does not feel dowdy in last season's hat? Others were undoubtedly bought to match an occasion—an outing, a wedding, a holiday, a business appointment, when it was important to feel at one's best. Others again, it is pretty certain, found their way into a personal hat-box because of a dull day, or dull mood. Many a woman will honestly own up when depressed, nothing helps to raise her spirits like a new hat. Call this a weakness if you like.

Men know something of it, too, though they may express it in a different way. 'It has always been my habit when I am worried by financial problems,' says Compton Mackenzie, 'to buy something. A defiant piece of extravagance is a tonic for such a mood. So I decided to order a new suit' —recording his reactions on a drenching day. The cost of one suit would normally cover that of several hats. And there may well be other motives; I do not pretend to know what moves Jane Morgan the American singer. Shortly before arriving in London, she was awarded the Golden Hat of the Year prize—as her country's best-hatted woman. She confessed to owning four hundred and fifty. She is in a class by herself.

A lot of nonsense has been written about hats in church. Nowadays, of course, even bishops lean over backwards to make it possible for a woman to go to worship without one. Invitations to this effect appear on noticeboards. In some instances, a little wisp of silk scarf is welcomed as a compromise.

This all goes back, of course, to Paul, and his instructions concerning the worshipping women of Corinth (I Cor. 11: 13). A great deal of business may well have been added to the hat-makers' trade by the literal interpretation of his words up through the years till now; but a great deal of harm has been done to an honest understanding of the purpose and spirit of his utterance. Only immodest women, whose character and conduct could not bear examination appeared in public at the time with heads uncovered. And the Christian worshipper needed to be careful about the details of her witness. As Dr William Barclay reminds us today: 'We must read this chapter not in the light of the twentieth century but in the light of the first century ... Corinth was probably the most licentious city in the world; and Paul's point of view was that in such a situation it was far better to err on the side of being too modest and too strict rather than to do anything which might either give the heathen a chance to criticize the Christians, or which would be a cause of temptation to the Christians themselves.'

We live in the twentieth century!

O Lord of Life, in all things let me display a surer sense of values today than seemed possible yesterday. Show me how life might be enriched. Amen.

Browse—or Drowse

I CHUCKLED as I saw it—a notice in one of the friendliest bookshops I know: *Browsers welcome—high browse or low browse*.

A book-lover ought also, I feel, to be a book-*buyer*. The public library can do much for one, but nothing makes up for owning, reading and re-reading. Even in this age of wireless and TV in so many homes, the old saying still stands: 'A room without books is a body without a soul.' Mr Churchill never more revealed his genius than when he urged architects in Britain's post-war years to plan for a built-in bookcase in every working-class home.

If we are not to surge on like dumb, driven cattle, at the mercy of mass propaganda, we must read. Cold print is better than hot air. If we are to escape drabness, boredom, discontent, and know colour, excitement and purpose in our days, we must read. If we are to know the most fascinating personalities of all times, the wisest, the most successful, we must read. If we are to move in a wide world, and not reject our richest heritage of mind and spirit, or refuse our place in the breath-taking advance of this age, we must read.

Every mother owes it to her growing family. Happy that youngster who later can say:

> *I had a mother who read me lays*
> *Of ancient and gallant and golden days . . .*
> *You may have tangible wealth untold:*
> *Caskets of jewels and coffers of gold:*
> *Richer than I you can never be—*
> *I had a mother who read to me.*

Again and again I meet people—usually busy housewives

49

in the thirty to forty age-group—who say, 'When the children are off my hands', or 'When I retire from the office in a year or two, I'm going to have a good read.'

I look at them, and as tactfully as I know how, ask: 'Do you have a good read now? If you don't squeeze it in somehow, you won't manage it then. You won't know what is available to read; you'll have lost the faculty; you'll be tired—as soon as you settle to follow a line of print, you'll drowse.'

Likewise every man owes it to himself to keep alive—and how better can he do that than by reading? When I use that term, I mean selective reading. 'Breathless thrillers' and 'bosom-claspers' have their place; but 'the eternal triangle' can be as boring as some people's 'family circle'.

I heard Dr Frank Laubach say something that has kept its place in the forefront of my mind ever since. In speaking of the millions newly come to literacy in this age he predicted: '*Whatsoever is sown in their minds, the world will reap.*'

What possible advantage can it be to us to have been born in this twentieth century, in a country where literacy is high, where presses turn out books unsurpassed in appearance since the world began—if we don't read? We might as well have been born to grovel in the fourteenth century, before William Caxton. It is not without significance that when he introduced the use of movable type, he set up his press in the precincts of the Church: the title-pages of his earliest volumes bear the location sign: 'In the Abbey of Westminster'.

Every literate Christian today, is surely answerable to God for what daily use he or she makes of books!

Deliver me this day from all laziness that contents itself with half-truths, half-understood. Amen.

H.M.V.

LATELY I came upon the end-of-garden grave of a little mongrel called 'Spot'. Nobody knew him beyond the home where he lived, and the few streets of his young master's paper-run. Yet he was dearly loved.

All round the world I have come upon such head-stones —some of them remembering famous animals, 'Greyfriars Bobby', outside the old church of that name in Edinburgh; another in the end of Carlyle's garden in Cheyne Row, Chelsea. But no memorial marks the grave of the most publicized dog—that little back-and-white terrier associated with His Master's Voice gramophone records. All that is known is that he was buried beside a mulberry bush in Eden Street, Kingston-upon-Thames, in Surrey, some sixty years ago. 'Nipper' belonged to the Barraud family of Liverpool, one of whom was an artist. Whenever the gramophone was played, he noticed how the dog sat peering wistfully into the round horn of the machine. Struck by his pose, he painted his portrait—little dreaming that it would become a trade-mark familiar to millions of us round the world.

But that is what has happened. The phonograph—with its first record of vibrations played back to reproduce sounds—invented by Thomas A. Edison was through its most painful teething-stages. Apart from demonstrations in Germany, and in England, by agents of the original firm, little interest in the surprising invention seems to have been shown, until two Frenchmen, Charles and Emil Pathé recognized it as a means of attracting clients to their tavern. But it did not stop at that. In time, William Barry Owen—in 1897, to be exact—established a venture in England. Two years later, Owen purchased the original painting of

'Nipper' listening to the phonograph, to which the name 'His Master's Voice' was given. This was first used as a trade-mark by the Victor Company, and about a decade later also by the Gramophone company trading under the famous initials H.M.V.

Today, no seal on any recording is better known—the old phonograph cylinder so easily broken, has of course, long since surrendered to the flat disc. But the little white terrier with his black ears sits listening intently, his nose all but in the horn. 'Everyone has seen the trade slogan "His Master's Voice",' as the modern theologian, Emil Brunner reminds us. And from mention of the little dog, he goes on to speak of something of lasting significance. 'If you buy a gramophone record,' he continues, 'you are told that you will hear the Master Caruso. Is that true? Of course! But really his voice? Certainly! And yet—there are some noises made by the machine which are not the master's voice, but the scratching of the steel needle upon the hard disc. But do not become impatient. For only by means of the record can you hear "the master's voice". *So, too, is it with the Bible. It makes the real Master's voice audible*—really His voice, His words, what He wants to say. But there are incidental voices accompanying, just because God speaks His word through the voice of man. Paul, Peter, Isaiah and Moses are such men. But through them God speaks His word. God has also come into the world as man, really God, but really *man*, too. Therefore the Bible is all His voice, not-withstanding all the disturbing things, which, being human are unavoidable. *Only a fool listens to the incidental noises when he might listen to the sound of his master's voice!* The importance of the Bible is that God speaks to us through it.'

Make Thy voice real to me today, O God, I beseech Thee—through the Bible, and in the quiet places of my heart and mind. Amen.

Right Here, Right Now

I MET a man a day or two ago whose hero is Cherry Garrard. I don't wonder at that. But I've not met anybody else who keeps his book, 'The Worst Journey In the World', above his work-bench.

He is a man of only moderate gifts, is married to a middle-aged wife, and minds a small business in one of the suburbs. No new building scheme is likely thereabouts—houses springing up overnight, crowded into less space than those built fifty years ago—so there is not the slightest prospect of his business suddenly expanding. Yet he seems to find shoe-mending rewarding—certainly he does a good job. And I don't know anybody in the area more loved; it's no bother to get a youngster to run a message to Mr Drew's shop, and many an old grandfather will sit and smoke a pipe with him.

I don't wonder that Mr Drew has made such a hero of Cherry Garrard. Do you remember how he sets down the secret of their expedition? 'All we could do was to put *one-foot-in-front-of-another-because-we-felt-the-journey-was-worth-it.*' I like that. I don't spend my days soaking leather and tapping away at shoes, nor trekking tirelessly hour after hour across the white spaces; but in between excitements, there are days and weeks when I need his secret. Anyone can start; starting power and staying power are not the same.

The most surprising poem that I've seen printed, was handed in to a paper I read regularly: perhaps you will say it isn't a poem. All it says is:

> *Go on, go on, go on, go on,*
> *Go on, go on, go on.*
> *Go on, go on, go on, go on,*
> *Go on, go on, go on.*

Strictly, I think you're right—it isn't a poem—but doesn't it hammer home a secret? My first impulse was to show it to Mr Drew; but I don't need to.

In the Book of Kings is a judgement on a man that I never understood till lately. Ordered to strike the ground, the record is that 'he struck three times, and stopped' (II Kings 13: 18). At first sight, he seems to have been rather hardly treated; he was ordered to strike, and he did three times— ah, but then he stopped! He started well enough, but he didn't keep on. In the New Testament Paul lays the same charge against the Galatians: 'You were running well: who hindered you?' (Gal. 5: 7, *R.S.V.*).

Running is one thing—it carries a certain impetus within itself—walking doesn't have that. So my admiration for Cherry Garrard grows, almost to that of Mr Drew; there is something splendid about being able to put one foot before another because one feels the journey is worth it.

Running and walking are strikingly tied together in that glorious promise to those who wait upon God: 'They shall run,' it says, 'and not be weary: they shall walk and not faint' (Isa 40: 31). And the second part seems the more relevant. Most of us—living the daily lives we do—mending shoes, preparing meals, wrapping parcels, attending to ledgers, patiently explaining verbs and adjectives to a class, know that what we need more than anything is the power to 'put one foot in front of another' on this most glorious journey on which we are set.

Happily, the promise still holds!

I bless Thee, Lord of Life, for the light of this new day; for home and loved ones, for work to do and strength to do it. Deliver me this day from all forms of dullness, and lack of faith. For Thy Name's sake. Amen.

On Bended Knees

I'VE spent a whole hour this morning on my bended knees—no, not praying—*weeding*. I won't say I haven't done a little praying as well; both are elementary occupations—there never was a human who didn't pray, or a garden that didn't produce weeds.

J. Kendal says:

> *I bet Adam cursed*
> *A bit at fursed*
> *When the Garden of Eden*
> *Wanted weeden.*

That's not the only thing the book of Genesis forgets to tell us; but we have not progressed further than the story of Job's struggles, when we are faced with 'foul weeds for barley' (Job 31: 40, Moffatt). And set down fairly in the first book of the New Testament, is the Master's realistic story of the 'weeds among the wheat' (Matt. 13: 25, Moffatt).

'The gardener must not be slothful,' wrote Walafred Strabo, monk of St Gall's monastery, in what is counted the first gardening-book ever, '*but full of zeal continuously.*' What a picture it gives of broken finger-nails, broken backs and sore knees. And from the Garden of Eden to this hour in my garden, there is nothing to be gained from refusing to recognize that this is the way things are.

In Tudor times 'weeding women' performed the ageless task in the King's Garden at Hampton Court. Its elaborate arbour-topped mounts, trellis-edged beds, and ingenious knottes enjoyed no immunity denied Adam, Job, the Galilean wheat-grower, good brother Walafred Strabo, or any garden-lover. The Palace rolls disclose the names of some fifteen to twenty such women, whose poor reward was twopence to threepence a day, with free meals of bread, herrings, and 'other things', washed down with ale. 'To root up unprofitable herbs,' they were fitted with stout leather gloves, iron-tipped like talons.

And the struggle goes on to this day, so that the precious hour spent on my bended knees this morning, armed with a broken dinner-knife, leaves little more than a momentary gap in those 'unprofitable herbs' waiting to be rooted out.

I was surprised a little time ago to learn of a 'Weed Show' that a group of garden-lovers put on. That still seems to me the highest form of charity. But one point at least it made clear—*that weeds are plants out of their proper place*. The show was a revelation to many who attended. A sprig of a plant like Queen Anne's lace—counted a choice flower in many places—was a weed in others. Soil and climate governing control seemed to have a good deal to do with it.

It sets one thinking of qualities that grow in the human spirit. Is *thrift* in one life, the weed, *miserliness*, in another? Is *timidity* in one climate *temerity* in another? Is it possible that the weed *harshness* is a flower that happens to be growing in a bitter soil? Is *sentimentality* a flower out of its proper place, or is it always a rank weed?

Lord Jellicoe spoke lately in the House of Commons about 'the growing weed of juvenile delinquency'. But could it be that even this growth, early and properly handled, might flower in daring, creative genius, and community service?

What makes a flower, a flower? And a weed, a weed?

Eternal Gardener, nurture within my spirit this day, things beautiful and true and of good report. Show me how to be generous in Love and instant in service. Amen.

Travellers

ONCE tie a label on your luggage—and set off by car, plane, train, donkey-cart, camel-train, ship—and life is never the same again. It can't be. Every person you meet, every magazine and paper you pick up, every item of news over the air has a new significance.

At one time travel was attended by all manner of hazards. A proverb claimed, 'There are three states of misery— sickness, fasting and travel.' One brave, or foolhardy enough to set off for unknown parts, was advised 'to pay all debts, provide for dependents, give parting gifts, return all articles under trust, take money and good temper for the journey; then bid farewell to all.'

But travel isn't as hazardous today; there are a thousand 'helps' to hand—travel agencies solicitous of patronage, with knowledgeable staff, and stacks of printed leaflets; not to mention friends and slight acquaintances who have travelled, whose one desire, it seems, is to see others do likewise. Alone, or in company, the greater part of the known world lies before one.

Some of us feel that a companion is essential—to help map an itinerary; to hold personal 'extras' whilst one presents one's passport; to struggle with a strange language; to share a meal, a joke, an unexpected pleasure. Others of us like to travel alone—to accept risks, judge character, and enjoy what each day brings.

Either way, it's a glorious enrichment. To see strange places, famous places, beautiful places; most of all to meet the people who belong in such places—to see what they look like, and to learn a little of what they make of life. Somebody said to Ella K. Maillart, travelling in Eastern Turkey: 'You will surely be sent back. Anyhow, whatever you do, don't ask questions.' To this she replied: 'But travelling is questioning!'

And it is—on a Cook's tour, on one's own feet, even *armchair travel that one takes at home*. For in talk of travel, this is by no means to be overlooked. It is the only travel possible to many—and to us all, when we haven't the time or the money to tie on the labels—a great standby. Psychologists can call it 'wish-fulfilment', 'dream-sublimation' or anything else they like. Let winds howl at the chimney-pots, rain assault our window-panes, there is not the least need to move an inch from where one sits snug in one's chair. The last train may have gone—but what does it matter? The world has no inn that will refuse us entry, no mountain-peak where we may not stand; no strange beauty, story or dance that we may not share. One who wrote:

> *Today I walked along an English lane*
> *Fragrant with perfume where the white May spills . . .*

had the secret. '*And yet,*' she adds, letting us into it, '*I did not stir beyond these walls of home!*'

A knowledge of the usage of twenty-six English letters, a heart wide open, a mind lightened, and a lively imagination are all that is needed. With no more money in the pocket than it takes to go to the public library, to one's favourite bookshop, or to the friendly shelf an arm's length away, this is travel open to everyone. 'Armchair travel'—if you will give it a commonplace name—the thing itself will never be commonplace.

But there is one book which asks *for more* than imaginative participation. As Dr Halford Luccock says strikingly: 'The Bible is about a journey: it is not addressed to the armchair traveller.'

God, I bless Thee for the majesty of this great Universe. But greater than Thy might, Thou hast shown me Thy mercy, more encompassing than Thy Law, Thy love. Amen.

A Rough Crossing

MERE mention of the English Channel is enough to send some of us green. Certainly it is enough to move us to sympathy for Louis of France. He also had a rough crossing. King or commoner, that little strip of water—twenty to thirty fathoms deep till it doubles that depth in the Strait of Dover—has never, it seems, been a respecter of persons. I have more than theoretical certainty of this. The Channel has long been temperamental, with winds mostly westerly, gales occurring chiefly between October and January, and fogs common throughout the year. Added to that, 'tides are peculiar,' I am informed by one possessed of extensive knowledge—though this piece of dispassionate observation helped me not at all in my crossing—'parts of the English coast having a double tide, the effect generally being to cause higher tides on the French coast with forty-two feet at St Germain, whilst on the English coast it is a matter of seven feet at Portland.'

In his little wooden ship, Louis of France made such an unhappy crossing, that in one part of it, serious doubt entered his mind on the matter of survival; but fortunately, the storm abated after a time, and as the vessel rose out of the trough of the waves, Louis rose from his despair. A little later, he was sufficiently himself to send for the master-mariner to ask the name of the wind that had caused them such distress. 'It was no great wind, Sire,' came the surprising answer, 'not one of the major winds of the world, not one of the cardinal winds, but a little side wind that hardly had a name.' Exactly!

Few of us suffer most from the great winds that blow in life; when they blow, we find ourselves possessed of unexpected reserves to meet them. That seems always to have

59

been a law of life. Ezekiel's wife dies—'the delight of his eyes'—and everybody expects him to be at once cast down and wordless. But Ezekiel rises to meet this sorrow in the midst of his public service with true nobility. Looking back later, he sets down his secret in a simple but superb statement: 'I spoke to the people in the morning, and at evening my wife died. And on the next morning I did as I was commanded' (Ezek. 24: 18).

Life's great tests find us with unexpected reserves—the death of one near and dear, a major operation, a community calamity, a national disaster. *Danger lies for us not in the great winds, but in the little side wind hardly worth a name.* Self-pity, pettiness, meanness, resentment, these are our undoing. A word 'slips out', a criticism is made, a promise is forgotten. The sudden challenge of a medical verdict finds us adequate, where as a sniffly cold in the head finds us full of complaint. Charles Lamb shows himself one of the most lovable characters, and one of the most heroic—except when he has a common cold. In his handling of his sister, 'mad Mary', no man could have been greater—but with a cold, no man more pitiable.

The young French thinker Comte de Saint-Simon had his valet wake him morning by morning with the words: 'Get up, monsieur le comte. Remember you have great things to do!' But it is not the 'great things'—the great winds—but the little seemingly insignificant things that test us out, the little side winds that hardly have a name.

Swift as I am to see the weaknesses of others, grant me the grace to handle my own, this day. Amen.

A Lash for Laziness

LENT is more than a lash for laziness laid on by the Church for forty days. As such, it might do something for those among us who during the remainder of the year neglect public worship and private devotion, but its worth would be limited.

The word itself comes from the Old English 'lencten' meaning Spring, *new life*. It is true, in the early centuries the Church did set a period of rigid fasting, and by the eighth or ninth century determined that it should begin on Ash Wednesday. Between that and Easter Day stretch forty days, excluding Sundays—which make up the period of Lent as we know it. But the emphasis is still on new life; so Lent, in its fullest, most meaningful sense, can never be an external thing.

The beloved George Herbert, poet and saint of the seventeenth century, understood it aright when he cried eagerly, 'Welcome, deare feast of Lent!' To him it meant richer life. And that should be its meaning for us.

Unhappily, many seem to have made it an external, petty observance—a cutting off of sweets, a reduction of cigarettes, a limiting of library books. One can't help noticing, in many cases, the result of this brief discipline is as likely to be self-inflation as self-denial. Lent is a lot more than feeling in the Jack Horner spirit, 'What a good boy am I!'

Some things, legitimate in themselves, may well be given up for the time being—as a sign that one's will is one's own, to consecrate to Christ—but the end is not the act in itself, *but life*. Mastery over one's bodily passions and appetites ought not to be left to a brief forty days a year.

It needs to be said also, that our Lord in no way disparaged daily material enjoyments of life. His enemies fastened on

His natural attitude to them, to dub Him 'gluttonous' and 'a wine bibber'. Details of the life of His immediate disciples are rare enough, so that there is no record of their fasting. Fasting is not an external sign of merit in itself—rather is it a stroke for freedom of spirit, more than ever necessary in these days of bodily comfort, even cloying luxury.

A little systematic belt tightening—provided it is not ostentatious—is good, but Lent provides us with an opportunity to do something a good deal more costly in its contribution to life. We need to sort out our priorities, to examine our loyalties, to step more often out of the centre of the mental picture of success that we are for ever building-up, to be more out-reaching to people we 'don't like', as well as being ready to cut out for a set number of days sugar and the things we 'do like'.

> *Now let the body fast awhile,*
> *The shelf and board grow lean,*
> *And man lift up his hungry heart*
> *To find a world unseen.*

Lent affords us this chance. Self-denial properly understood is less a matter of 'things' than of spirit, because its end is Life.

So, having 'closed the door', as our Lord instructed—to shut out the pressures of the world and its flattery—let us kneel and simply and sincerely pray: 'From all blindness of heart; from pride, vain-glory and hypocrisy; from envy, hatred, malice and all uncharitableness, Good Lord, deliver us!'

Gracious Lord, everywhere present, I bless Thee for what I know of life, in Thee. Let Thy spirit move the thoughts of my mind and the purpoess of my heart. Amen.

Another Matter

As Good Friday approaches, preparation for presenting what Professor T. W. Manson calls 'the central thing', may hold no problems for preachers and leaders of adult groups, but for those of us who must keep this holy time with little children, it is another matter. From the start, he reminds us, 'the central thing was not the Sermon on the Mount, but the Cross on the Hill.'

Now how are we to convey this to little children? To them, Death in any form, is a forbidding subject. The little child spoke for many, who said: 'I wish it wasn't *called* that. I don't think I should mind so much if it were called "*Hig*".'

Well, it isn't called that—and the cruellest form known to men of His day, meted out to the Friend of little children Who gathered them about Him, and blessed them, when the adults would have driven them away, is still called 'Death'.

What are we parents and teachers to do about it? You have your own solution of the problem, perhaps. Do you remember the reference to the Crucifixion in Richard Jefferies' book, *Bevis, the Story of a Boy*? 'The Crucifixion hurt his feelings very much, the cruel nails, the unfeeling spear; he looked at the picture a long time, and then turned the page saying, "If God had been there He would not have let them do it!".' But that only adds another problem to the one that already exists—God *was* there, and He let them do it!

Even to hear the record of it read, as set out in the Gospels, is too much for some children. In the *Life of Florence Barclay*—a favourite author of novels when some of us were children, or just growing into novel readers—is an instance. It occurred on the Good Friday after her fourth birthday, this unforgettable impression. 'The family were in Church ... No doubt Benny (as they called her) had been playing with the hymn-books and hassocks as was her wont. But when it came to the reading of the Gospel for the day, her mother stood her up on her seat. The passage was, of course, the account of the Passion, according to St John.' The little girl's father, the preacher, had a beautiful and impressive way of reading. All went well at the start— the simplicity of the evangelist's style and the deep, grave voice of her father gained her attention. Soon, she was completely absorbed. She heard how Judas betrayed, how Peter denied, and the servant was struck his blow. Then followed the long interview with Pilate. Breathlessly, she listened. What would he do? Jesus, of whom she had eard a lot, and loved, stood before him. Her eyes never eft her father's calm, kind face. Surely Pilate would be kind, too. 'The story proceeded. How dare they mock Him! How *could* they shout that He should be crucified! Still, Pilate was trying to save Him—oh, surely, he would. Then suddenly came the terrible truth. It was too much for Benny. Sinking down on the seat of the old square pew, she burst into a paroxysm of weeping. "*Why* did they—*why* did they?" she sobbed. "*Oh, mother, why did they?*"'

Adult members of that congregation were, like many of us, hearing with unflinching calm, the familiar record of earth's most crucial moment, when God's Son stood arraigned before men—but for a little child hearing the record of it for the first time, *it was too much.*

Now what are we to do? A little child cannot be expected to bear such a sense of calamity—we must do two things, I think—*spare as much as we can the harrowing details, and link the whole sad event with the 'happy ending', the glorious triumph of Easter Day!*

For every wonder of the living Gospel, I bless Thee, O Lord, this day. Amen.

Gloriously Wrong

ONE of the smallest words in our language, and one of the most dangerous is the word 'end'; and when it is made to keep company with 'dead', it is doubly so. One can be so gloriously wrong. John Moore tells of a notice-board which someone put up in his village some time ago: DEAD END— to River, Inn and Church. The parson objected, and it was taken down. I don't wonder. No one can rightly claim to be as positive as that.

There is no forgetting Peter. Have you noticed how Matthew's gospel records that dramatic turn in events? To the amazement of those men who followed Him, Jesus had been betrayed, and immediately made a prisoner. Next moment He was being led away. It was night there in the Garden of cruel shadows. And His disciples, scattering in fear, let Him go. 'But Peter,' the record says, 'followed afar off unto the High Priest's palace ... to see the end' (Matt. 26: 58).

At this distance of place and time, it is easy to look at the matter differently; but to Peter, it looked like the end; the end, not only of a stimulating three-year companionship in village and city and out under the stars, but the end of that lovely Life. And that meant the end of those stories to which the common people had listened gladly; the end of those gracious glimpses of a fuller knowledge of God; the end of all those miraculous cures; the end of all their hopes. Peter was utterly shocked, and bewildered.

But, of course, Peter was wrong—and he was one of the first to know it. On that never-to-be-forgotten morning, following the anguish and ignominy of the trial and crucifixion, and the laying away of the beloved Body, the message came beside an open Tomb: 'Go tell His disciples, and Peter.'

In no time, in that very city where these things occurred, men and women—for three days utterly cast down—possessed now with a new and unbelievable courage, were claiming that He was alive. More than that, that they had seen Him. It was all so unlike anything they had experienced before, that one of their number, Thomas, even refused to believe it. But in a face-to-face encounter with his Living Lord, even his excusable doubt had to give way. It was so different from 'the end' that Peter envisaged.

And the surprise of it still holds; Bernard Shaw, in one of his prefaces, sets it down strikingly for us in words of our day: 'An angel opened the family vault of Joseph, a rich man of Arimathea, who had buried Jesus in it; whereupon Jesus rose and returned from Jerusalem to Galilee and resumed His preaching with His disciples, assuring them that He would be with them to the end of the world. At that point,' adds Shaw, 'the narrative abruptly stops. The story has no ending.'

In this nuclear age, some among us are slow to know this shining truth, in its full historical, experimental, life-making sense. To the rest of us, words spoken before ever He drew human breath, and started on the way that led eventually to the open Tomb, with its glorious triumph over Death, and Ascension, have increasing significance: 'Thou shall call His name Jesus . . . and of His Kingdom there shall be no end.'

> *Speak, History! Who are life's victors?*
> *Unroll the long annals and say. . . .*

O Lord, give to all who must make important decisions this day, a clear sense of Thy will. For Christ's sake. Amen.

Interruptions

PEOPLE on party lines get the blame for a big share of life's annoyances. I happen to be on a party-line. But interrupted conversations can't all be attributed to the same cause. Subscribers living in the neighbourhood of Cranham, Gloucestershire, must have been surprised lately to learn, when investigations were made, that the tiresome interruptions they suffering continually were due to squirrels chewing through the new polythene cables to get at the insulating fat.

It is a pleasant relief to have squirrels to blame; though people on party-lines, and people in all sorts of other situations, I am afraid, must still bear their share of blame for most of our interruptions.

Oliver Wendell Holmes begins one of his books with the familiar statement: '*I was just going to say, when I was interrupted* . . .' One of the most famous interruptions in literature must be that of the man who knocked on the door when Coleridge was intent on his 'Kubla Khan'. We have no idea of his name; he is referred to always as 'the man from Porlock'. But the poet himself has left us in no doubt about the devastating nature of that interruption. 'The author,' he says, 'continued for about three hours in a profound sleep. On awakening he appeared to himself to have a distinct recollection of the whole, and taking pen, ink and paper, instantly and eagerly wrote down the lines that are here preserved. At this instant he was unfortunately called out by a person on business from Porlock, and detained by him above an hour, and on his return to the room, found, to his no small surprise and mortification, that . . . with the exception of some eight or ten scattered lines and images, all the rest had passed away.'

67

One can't but be furious with that 'man from Porlock'. What did he want? Was he collecting a bill? I've been to Porlock; it's a small place, tucked away. And one can't escape the feeling that his business was small business, though it took 'above an hour'. The length of the interruption is nothing to go by—some people can spin out the smallest matter. We've heard them—on the telephone, at the door. It makes no difference whether one is beginning a book like Holmes, or a poem like Coleridge—or a pie, a morning's spring-cleaning, a sermon for Sunday, which is much more likely to be your lot and mine. Something has to be done about interruptions. It's no use getting mad about them; they are going to be with us as long as life lasts.

More than that, *Death itself is an interruption*. It was that to our Lord. You remember His words: 'Yet a little while I am with you, *and then* . . .' (John 7: 33; John 13: 33). The fellowship so precious between Him and His disciples wouldn't be ended by that grim Cross—only interrupted. It wasn't to be expected that those earth-born men to whom He spoke would understand it: but they did afterwards. On the first Easter morn in a garden, He met Mary, and picked up again that interrupted fellowship; later He met Peter and John and the rest. No wonder John sets down, with new significance, another reference to 'a little while', ending with a glorious certainty concerning the 'interruption' we call Death: 'Yet a little while, and the world seeth Me no more; but ye see Me: because I live, ye shall live also' (John 14: 19).

This is the basis of our continuing confidence that Life is all of a piece, though early or late, it will be interrupted.

O Lord, I rejoice that Thy love which cannot let me off, is also Thy love which will not let me go. Amen.

It all Depends

I KNEW a dozen or more doors like it once, with panes of glass—ruby, harsh blue and white—not to mention porch windows turned conservatories. I'd almost forgotten their existence, till I came upon an old house in a side street today that had somehow missed the on-going tides of life. As a child, I longed to have such a house—but never did. An old neighbour who spent an hour each morning pottering away at her plants behind such glass, roused my envy. An old man I knew used to sit in a little patch of tinted sunlight, sucking away at his pipe.

In the opening of his story of the *Parish of Crainie*, J. W. Stevenson tells of the meeting of the minister and his people. 'I saw them first,' says he, 'through the tinted glass of the vestry window; in the blue I could see only the blurred outline of their faces, in the red every feature—an anticipation of how some were to be known to me almost with the certainty of heaven's face-to-face, and others were to be mistakenly judged.

'They moved into the old church on the Knowe to take their vows; perhaps not reckoning, many of them, on all that it meant to be bound to a minister, as I certainly did not reckon on what would happen to me because I was bound to them.'

Christ's word, 'Judge not, that ye be not judged' (Matt. 7: 1), used to worry me quite a lot, until I realized that the word 'judge' has many meanings. Discrimination and concern for worth-while values are essential; worthy conduct is all important. But the word 'judge' means also censoriousness, and carries the hint of a prosecuting attorney. And it is in this sense that it is 'out' for us, living in the Parish of Crainie, or in the community we know best, working in the Church, where Sunday gathers us in with others to worship. With the best will in the world, we see them one by one through little panes of coloured glass— some heightening our judgement, some obscuring it. *It is so easy to be mistaken.*

None of us has material enough on which to make an irrevocable judgement—*none of us.*

There was a day in Crainie's Scotland, when King George the Fifth talked with John Wheatley, Member for Clydeside. Asked why he was such a revolutionary, expressing his convictions so violently, he simply recalled to the king something of the slums with which he was familiar and the life of the people there, cursed by conditions and the dark spectre of unemployment. When he had finished, the king said quietly: 'If I had seen what you have seen, I too would be a revolutionary.' *The little pane of glass through which one looks makes such a difference.* I wish I could say I always remember this; but being a human creature, it's not easy.

Paul faced it in his own place and time. The right that he allowed his fellows and himself is one that I must handle for my fellows and myself in the same way. Says he: 'It is a very small thing that I should be judged of you, or of man's judgment . . . *He that judgeth me is the Lord*' (I Cor. 4: 3-4).

Loving Lord, I rejoice in the possibility that life today may be a splendid thing. Grant me a loving heart, O Lord, and a kind tongue. Amen.

Meet a Saint

FOR the young person in your family, what is your greatest single wish? 'The greatest ambition I have for my boy,' said Dr Roger Lloyd, 'is that he should *meet a saint.*'

Surprising? No, not really. Merely proof that this good modern father is not as silly as some of us, and knows what he means by a saint. He is not thinking of an ascetic with thin feet in sandals and his head in a halo. Not at all. To meet such a person would be more likely to repulse a healthy boy, setting out in life, than quicken his heart-beat, add to his joy and strengthen his courage. To learn from Paul that as Christians 'of the Church of God', we are *'called to be saints'* (I Cor. 1:2) might not help, either. For some, the very word 'saint' conjures up an age gone by, with gibbet, thumb-screw and burning faggots; of men and women with pale faces, who chose to retire from this sinful world's battles, to fasting, self-mortification, and prayers.

It is plain that Roger Lloyd has come freshly to this lovely New Testament word; and to those carrying it forward through Time, 'the luminous trail of saints whom Christ has made.' 'The mark of a saint,' he knows as clearly as Bishop Westcott, 'is not perfection but consecration'—not a person without fault, but one who has given himself without reserve to God. He has lifted the idea of sainthood out of its niche of pale piety, and has seen it for the splendid, rich thing it is—in daily living, walking up and down the world, with mind alert, and hands out-reached in service that counts. God is always fashioning His world through people like this. 'It is impossible to measure,' writes the historian, Professor Butterfield, in his *Christianity and History*, 'the vast difference that ordinary Christian piety has made to the last two thousand years of European history.' He goes on to describe it as 'the most moving spectacle that history presents.'

This is the sort of person the doctor wants his son to meet —one in our day, showing the spirit of 'Saint' Wilfred Grenfell of Labrador, 'Saint' Mildred Cable of the Gobi Desert, 'Saint' Dick Sheppard of St Martin's, 'Saint' John Baillie of his lecture-room, 'Saint' Howard Somervell, half-way up Everest, 'Saint' Alice Sargent, scrubbing out St Catherine's Church, Nottingham, 'Saint' Tom, 'Saint' Dick, 'Saint' Harry on the scaffolding of a building-job, or at the docks, or busy with head-bowed at a desk or serving across a counter in the High Street.

'It is possible,' says Dr Murdo Macdonald, 'that the Church today produces as many saints as she has ever done in any previous epoch of her history. They are, however, not so easily recognized, nor are they so eagerly venerated. The explanation for this new evaluation,' he adds, 'is complex, but one reason is that the contemporary mind has fastened on *secular* substitutes which have won the admiration and called forth the adulation of the masses.' Saints are not much skilled in self-advertisement.

But a challenge shimmers through those splendid words. The greatness of Christianity is seen less in its creeds and councils than in its saints. They are not made suddenly, but make real the living spirit of Christ, in our world; and where they are, things never remain as they were before. They see God, and know Him as the Great Reality; they rejoice in their devotion, and live in daily service to their fellows, for His sake.

Never a day passes, but I *meet such a saint. Your boy may, too, and your girl!*

O Lord, teach me to live. Let all my earning, my spending, my saving and giving meet with Thine approval and blessing. And lighten my step with laughter. Amen.

Spring o' the Year

THE miracle is upon us again! Newspaper headlines are ominous enough, but it makes little difference. One may be forgiven for echoing Gilbert Thomas, one of our present day poets:

> *I thought that God perchance, in punishment*
> *Of the world's sin, would stay His gifts this year—*
> *And that no Spring in glory would appear—*
> *Even His mercy must, it seemed, be spent!*
> *Yet, on this blue May morning as I went*
> *Along the rustling lanes, the birds made cheer*
> *Such as before had never charmed my ear;*
> *And had the wood e'er breathed a richer scent?*
> *So sweet it was I fled! I could not face*
> *The scourge of God's forgiveness! I could bear*
> *Amid the world's red guilt and black despair;*
> *'Thy wrath,' I cried, 'but not Thy mercy, Lord!*
> *'Oh, spare me from the year's unfolding grace,*
> *'For every flower is as a two-edged sword!'*

Whilst Nature is being gloriously transformed, let the call of the renewing love of God come to us. From the very beginning of time, God has hinted at this miracle: 'Remember ye not the former things,' He says to His people. 'Behold I will do a new thing: now it shall spring forth' (Isa. 43: 18-19). Paul, carrying it forward confidently into the New Testament period of time, cries: 'If any man be in Christ he is a new creature: old things are passed away; behold all things are become new' (II Cor. 5:17). Nor does this miracle-bearing note end here; it is carried forward to be part of the ultimate triumph. In the Book of the Revelation are the words beloved above all others by Temple Gairdner in our day—

one of the choicest spirits to pass through Trinity College, Oxford. The morning after he acknowledged the Lordship of Christ, he ordered an illuminated text for his wall, bearing those very words: 'Behold, I make all things new' (Rev. 21: 5). Whilst the world about us is rejoicing in life and beauty after the winter's stubborn seige, this is the message to meet our hearts.

So easily do we become worn and bedraggled by care, so easily soiled, that nothing short of the transforming forgiveness of God can meet us where we are.

Politics, as one of our leaders reminds us, can give us shortened hours of work, better living conditions, but 'politics merely accept man as he is in his natural position and character—the religious idea alone,' he has to add, 'has power to transform a man.'

This is the essential message of Christianity, and nothing in this modern day, for all our education, and technology, can take its place. It is our business to reiterate it, and interpret it, in terms that modern men and women can understand. If our hearts grown weary are to be transformed, and our poor, stumbling world made new, it must be by the mercy of God.

'*The function of the Church is to keep a Springtime freshness in the world!*'

O God, I rejoice in the rising of the Springtime sap. I bless Thee for the blood in my veins, and the strength in my arms. But greater than any gift of Nature, is Thy forgiveness and sustaining Love, through Christ my Saviour. Amen.

His Map

IT all started, I imagine, when a man broke off a piece of
stick and started drawing patterns in the dust. Perhaps a
neighbour needed some help at the outset of a journey—
directions to the next well, or something of that sort. When
the world's first permanent map was made, nobody knows;
the oldest extant are Babylonian clay tablets in the British
Museum, dating about 2,300 B.C. In their turn, the
Egyptians, as early as the time of Rameses II—about
1330–1300—were turning out very respectable maps. I can
think of few more stirring moments than when I was granted
the privilege of examining the earliest attempts now in the
British Museum.

Most of us have grown up with detailed maps in the back
of our Bibles; the strange thing is that the word 'map' does
not once appear within. This is not to suggest that there was
lacking at that time a knowledge of the local scene, or the
fascinating pull of the unknown. Not at all. But this must
have been restricted to the few. Abraham was only one
who, impelled from within, 'went out, not knowing whither
he went' (Heb. 11: 8). Palestine—birthplace of our Lord
—was quite a small country, only about the size of Wales.
From the Lebanon range, on the northern boundary, to the
deserts into which its high lands melted in the south was a
length of about one hundred and forty miles; its width from
the Mediterranean to the Jordan valley ranged from twenty-
five miles at the upper end to nearly eighty at the lower, with
twenty more added to cover the trans-Jordanian uplands.

But this was only the beginning; the Gospel proclaimed
first by our Lord, Who walked up and down that relatively
small piece of geography, was never to stay there. He made
that plain to His disciples. Following on His own ministry,

75

death, and resurrection, the time came for Him to exchange the limitations of His physical presence for His spiritual nearness. 'And they went forth, and preached everywhere,' the last verse in Mark's Gospel says, 'the Lord working with them, and confirming the word with signs following' (Mark 16: 20). But it all took time. That word 'everywhere', at that stage, doubtless meant as much of the world as was known at that time. Centuries later, men were still in the progressive stage. As one said with a smile—

Geographers in Afric maps
With savage pictures filled their gaps,
And o'er unhabitable downs
Placed elephants for want of towns.

Today we have an almost complete knowledge of the earth's surface and to some extent of the sea bottom.

In his *Life of Alexander the Great*, Harold Lamb tells of a great moment when the army, following that great conqueror, found they had *marched off the map*. The only maps they had were Greek maps, showing only a part of Asia Minor. Consternation reigned, and understandably so.

But this can't happen to us modern Christians—we serve a Lord whose commission has no geographical limits. His title is 'Christ, the Saviour of the world' (John 4: 42), and His word to us, 'Ye shall be witnesses unto Me both in Jerusalem, and in Judea, and in Samaria, and to the uttermost part of the earth' (Acts 1: 8).

We can't march off His map!

I rejoice, O Lord, that Thou hast called me to partnership in a large task. Amen.

Verbs are Hinges

WHAT could a Broadcasting Company's typist, set to list hymn-recordings, understand by it? Much less an announcer. The offending typist might argue that there was little space provided for a lengthy title. But when the man at the microphone announced that magnificent hymn of Herbert's, which I had chosen to be part of my broadcast, as: 'Let all the world!' I was at a loss. Without its *verb* it said nothing. I found myself longing for time enough to give its first verse in full:

> *Let all the world in every corner sing:*
> *My God and King!*
> *The heavens are not too high,*
> *His praise may thither fly;*
> *The earth is not too low,*
> *His praises there may grow.*
> *Let all the world in every corner sing:*
> *My God and King!*

If you are one who pays attention to such matters, there will be times when you are as painfully surprised. When the announcement of a hymn from a broadcast studio, or from a pulpit, reaches the ear as the one chosen that morning, it is not only slovenly, it is unintelligible.

Worse still, is the tendency of some among us *to drop the verb out of religion.* The New Testament on which we are meant to nourish our spirits, is full of verbs. It is impossible to turn a page without coming upon them—'Come!' 'Follow!' 'Go!' 'Do!' They are all there. And they must be as tellingly, clearly present in our day-to-day discipleship. 'What do ye more than others?' is one of our Lord's penetrating questions. Words are well enough in their place,

77

sung or spoken; but unless they lead out into action, they are of little worth in His sight. It was this that good John Lydgate understood, centuries ago, when he said: 'Woord is but wynd: leave woord and take the deede.'

The immortal story of the Jericho Road has never been forgotten—though by some, it appears, the main point of it has never been quite grasped. *It all hinges on its verbs;* and it is plain that our Lord meant it to. The Priest and the Levite were religious men, without doubt—but their religion didn't add up to much. It had no verbs. On their way to worship God, they each saw the beaten fellow on the roadside, but neither did anything for him. That was left to the outsider, the foreigner, the man the world now calls the Good Samaritan. Our Lord tells us very little about him; but what we do know is enough to make him immortal, and to provide to this hour a challenge—*his verbs were good!* Without thought of his own safety, or convenience, he did what he could immediately. Nor was that all—when the first-aid job was finished, he got the poor fellow to the inn; and when he had satisfied himself that he was comfortable, paid his reckoning. Nor did his care stop there—he knew he would be that way again, and if convalescence proved long, more would be forthcoming from his wallet to settle the charges. Those who listened first to that graphic word-picture never forgot it. Summed up, its pointed question is, *'How are your verbs?'*

Gracious Lord, cleanse my religion from selfishness and introspection, from wordy assent, and unwillingness to serve. Quicken my imagination, that I may know how things are with my fellows, and reach out my hand where I can help. Amen.

It Surprises Me

WE'VE got a new chair—not a shiny one direct from the furniture factory—really an old one. A friend, set to the onerous task of dismantling a family home, gave it to us. It goes by the name of 'Great-Grannie-Polly', that of the little lady whose property it once was. We like it. It has a gracious line; its upholstery matches well the room in which we have put it, and it is comfortable to sit in. Every little while, during the first day or two, we found ourselves suddenly dashing into the room, *to take it by surprise.* We got the idea from J. M. Barrie.

Do you remember his opening page in *Margaret Ogilvy*? 'On the day I was born,' he begins, 'we bought six hair-bottomed chairs, and in our little house it was an event ... I so often heard the tale afterwards, and shared as boy and man in so many similar triumphs, that the coming of the chairs seems to be something that I remember, as if I had jumped out of bed on that first day and run ben to see how they looked. I am sure my mother's feet were ettling to be ben long before they could be trusted, and that the moment after she was left alone with me she was discovered bare-footed in the west room, doctoring a scar (which she had been the first to detect) on one of the chairs, or sitting on them regally, or withdrawing and reopening the door suddenly to take the six by surprise.'

I've never felt inclined to laugh at her: I've had such fun out of new possessions by doing the same—'Great-Grannie-Polly' is only the latest.

It would be a pity if surprise should die out of life. Many a time I've seen one and another I know stand up in church and sing

> *I know not what the future hath*
> *Of marvel or surprise,*

79

as if it were the most prosaic thing in creation. I'm sure they have never 'taken their chairs by surprise'. And I am left wondering how they are going to get on in the future life, if they have shown so little surprise in this. For this world of God's is filled with surprise; He meant it to be so. Is He not the God who surprised Jacob, the runaway, till he rose up to say, 'Lo, God is in this place, and I knew it not?' Is He not the God Who spoke to Moses out of a burning bush as he shepherded a few sheep, till he found himself slipping off his shoes, because the place whereon he stood was holy?

This ought to have prepared men for the gift of His Son, and the surprise of His coming—but, of course, it didn't. 'Ye shall find a babe, wrapped in swaddling clothes, and lying in a manger.' And to pile surprise upon surprise, there was His growing up in Nazareth—a little place of no consequence. 'Did any good thing ever come out of Nazareth?' was a common saying. And what words can express the surprise of the Resurrection? Time had not dulled its bright edges, when one walking to Emmaus said: 'Some women of our number gave us a surprise' (Luke 24: 22, Moffatt). These had this news first—but isn't it still the world's best news?

'Expect surprises,' are George Morrison's words to us. 'Have an open eye. Believe that there are more things in heaven and earth than have been dreamed of in your philosophies!'

Almighty God, Whose thoughts are higher than any human mind can fully grasp, keep me awake to the surprises of Thy Kingdom. For Christ's sake. Amen.

An Uncomfortable Possession

THE small boy who defined 'conscience' as 'man's most uncomfortable possession', was not far from the truth. Just after the first World War, a young British officer who had been serving in Bensberg, West Germany, felt he'd like to carry away a souvenir with him. So he got the use of a tall ladder and climbed up a memorial, and from a wreath held by the Goddess of Peace, plucked a bronze leaf.

At the time, he felt pleased with himself; but in the years since—a successful business-man in New Zealand—his spirited prank began to lay heavily upon his conscience. A little while ago, it became possible for him to make a holiday trip back to Europe. Outstanding among his memories, is the moment when he returned to Bensberg—to *restore* the bronze leaf he had lifted from the memorial. In the forty-five years' interval, oddly, no one had noticed it was missing. But one young man—growing old and more responsible—was glad of the chance to get it off his conscience. Entering into the spirit of the undertaking, the townsfolk received him and his family as guests of the town.

Not all stories of conscience work out to such a happy ending. The most decisive battles this world knows, I suppose, are not fought on external battle-fields, but in men's consciences.

Kant, who wrote much on conscience, called this 'most uncomfortable possession' 'the categorical imperative'. If this sounds a mouthful, it needs only a moment's serious thought to know what he means. To start with, there is a real difference between Right and Wrong. Once the difference between these is seen, conscience commands one to avoid the one course and to follow the other. More than being an imperative, it is a 'categorical imperative'—it accepts no excuse. Often such action, of course, may be dead against one's inclinations, one's professional and social interests, indeed, against the advice offered by friends and family; but it makes no difference.

When all this is said—and it must be said—a point of great importance must be added, since conscience has sometimes been loosely called 'the voice of God within'. It is not; because it can sometimes *be wrong*. Paul discovered this; in his early life he considered it his duty to persecute Christians and oppose Christ, just as later he counted it his duty to suffer for Christ, as a Christian. In the first case, his conscience was honest; but he was mistaken, nevertheless. It is plain that conscience, like other faculties, must be *trained and sensitized*. A lot of painful experience lay behind Paul's striking words before his accusers: 'Herein do I exercise myself, to have always a conscience void of offence toward God, and toward men' (Acts 24: 16). One notices the order of procedure—first God, and then man.

'The test of a Church,' says Dr Hensley Henson in our own day, 'is the *kind of conscience* it creates in its members.' He is thinking of us less, I believe, as committee members, more as members of the community. This is important. Notice he does not make the test the kind of worship or the kind of creed, but the kind of conscience. Is he right? Is this the mark of the spirit of Christ within? Dr Harry Fosdick fashions this prayer for himself, and for those of us who will use it: 'Grant unto us more sensitive consciences. If we have sinned against those who trust us ... do Thou forgive us. Make us sensitive.'

O God of Truth and Goodness, in Thy Mercy this day, let all that is hollow and unreal in me be forgiven. Let me serve Thee with a pure heart—and glad. Amen.

A Canticle in the Bath

SHELLEY made an immortal poem about a skylark, Burns about a mouse, and Monet sat all day in front of one haystack painting it in its changing colours. These give me courage to publicly praise God for a bath—for what Rupert Brooke calls 'the benison of hot water'. I have just returned from a long journey tired, wet and cold.

To luxuriate in a hot bath is one of the commonplace benefits of living in the twentieth century. At one time, baths were found only in palaces—the Egyptians had them. Examples of those enjoyed in the palaces of the Aegean civilization are still with us—in Knossos and Phaistos, one's imagination is at a loss to feel what it was like to bathe seventeen-hundred years BC. The Greeks were not behind in this; and of course, the Romans developed the bath beyond anything dreamed of up to their time.

But no ordinary mortal like myself, at journey's end and at other times, as desire arose, knew this joy.

The beloved St Francis—in his Canticle—sang: 'Praise be my Lord for our sister Water, who is very serviceable unto us and humble and precious and clean.' But I can hardly think he meant hot water, or had in mind a bath, described quaintly in one learned work as 'the means of immersing the body in some medium other than atmospheric air for the purpose of cleanliness'. Cleanliness, I fear, wasn't next to godliness in St Francis' time. Indeed, there were saints of the Middle Ages who believed that to enter a bath was to pay undue attention to the body, and to encourage vanity. For centuries after St Francis sang, the situation was little changed.

A gossip in the time of the first Queen Elizabeth reported: 'The Queen hath built herself a bath, where she doth take herself every month, whether she require it or no.' Mary Queen of Scots, records tell us, bathed in wine, for which ritual she demanded and received an increased allowance. Madame Tallien, in her turn, favoured a bath of crushed raspberries. A sticky business, it seems far removed from the Canticle I would sing in praise of hot water! This is one of the good, ordinary things of home in this favoured century, and surely a fit subject for praise.

To turn a tap and have water issue forth—hot or cold—is a miracle. Nobody knows now the name of the man who invented the first tap. Or was it a woman? Certain it is, that for centuries, strong backs and sturdy arms have carried pails of water between copper and bath-tub, with an extra jug to regulate the temperature. Within living memory, undergraduates in some of the Oxford Colleges have taken their baths in this fashion. When the difficulties involved were ventilated at a College Meeting, one Master is remembered to have said, 'What do they want baths for? They're only up for eight weeks.'

Still, according to a newspaper report, between three and four million bathless homes remain in Britain. I find this a distressing thought—as distressing as the fact that many of us do enjoy daily 'the benison of hot water', without thanks to God. *Praise be my Lord for our sister Water, who is very serviceable unto us and humble and precious and clean.*

O God, there is no good and lovely thing except it come from Thee—and no true refreshment of body and spirit! Let no part of my life lack praise and thanksgiving. Let Thy Name be glorified in earth's common blessings! Amen.

On Hands and Knees

IT was my fault, I admit it. We had not been in Ambleside ten minutes, when amid its grey stone buildings, I found the one pictured on many calendars. It is unique—a tiny building on a bridge straddling a rushing stream, a charming place, safe for all time now, thanks to the National Trust.

The door stood open, and as it happened, an officer of the Trust was inside. He looked up at sound of our shoes on the stone steps. We assured him of our eager interest.

'It was a summer-house, with apple-trees growing by, three-hundred years ago,' said he. 'Some people still call it the "apple-house".

'How big is it actually?' I asked. And then felt it a foolish question. For, to my surprise, he answered, 'I don't know.' With that, he rummaged among some papers, pencils, rubbers and things, and came forth with a measure, murmuring the while about the details all being in the Deeds. Next moment, the two of us got down on our hands and knees. Its size proved to be nine feet one way, five feet six inches the other!

But as soon as I had the measurements I realized that one can't measure uniqueness that way. I shall never ask such a foolish question again. You can't measure a home in lineal inches—only in love; nor can you measure a church in terms of space—only in spirit. The Book of Ezekiel— between chapters 40 and 43—ought to be compulsory reading for all parsons, church-goers and critics. It is about the man who carried a measuring-reed into the place of worship. Long before he had it all lined up, he began to look pretty silly. 'For the glory of the Lord came into the house by the gate whose prospect is towards the east . . . and the glory of the Lord filled the house!'

It is just as foolish to attempt to measure God in the world in which we find ourselves. Modern man has achieved much; but not enough to be blasé even yet. One such declares:

> *God is a proposition,*
> *And we that prove Him are His priests, His chosen.*
> *From base hypotheses*
> *Of strata and wind, of stars and tides, watch me*
>   *construct His universe.*
> *A working model of my majestic notions,*
> *A sum done in the head,*
> *Last week I measured the light—His little finger.*
> *The rest is a matter of time.*

Oh, no, it's not! Learn this, little man with the measuring-rod, God's greatness and mystery are beyond you. You cannot even measure *man*, His creation—despite your laboratory talk of lime, carbon, magnesium and iron—*how then can you measure the Creator?* He Himself asks: 'Who is this that darkeneth counsel by words without knowledge? Where wast thou when I laid the foundations of the earth? Declare, if thou hast understanding. Who hath laid the measures thereof, if thou knowest? . . . Or who laid the corner stone thereof, when the morning stars sang together, and all the sons of God shouted for joy? Or who shut up the sea with doors, when it brake forth?' (Job 38).

Every reverent spirit knows the answer.

Almighty God, Creator of all things, grant me humility and awe when I behold the wonders of this great universe. And to Thy Name be the glory! Amen.

Not a Policeman

To step into London alone for the first time can be quite an experience. But few of us, if any, lack friends and fellow-travellers ready to offer advice. Distances may be hard to gauge, destinations difficult to locate, traffic bewildering, but one well-tried source of help still stands: 'When in doubt,' they say, *'ask a policeman.'* Directing the traffic in the busy thoroughfares, or appearing suddenly and silently in a moment of indecision, any one of the eleven hundred good men and true, of the City Force, or of the larger Metropolitan Police, extending over a radius of fifteen miles from Charing Cross, becomes a veritable godsend.

And no least sense of ingratitude is intended, when one goes on confidently to state a larger truth, in the words of the poet:

> *A thousand policemen directing the traffic*
> *Cannot tell you why you come or where you go.*

This is something that goes deeper, and extends further than the function of a policeman. It belongs to that larger area of enquiry covered by Lord Soper, in the open air, over the last forty years on Tower Hill. Many of us, visitors to London, as well as those spending their working years at its heart, know this historic spot near the Tower on its eastern rampart. At a midweek lunch-hour—paperbags, sandwich-packets in hand—we make up a lively crowd, gathered to listen and to question. After so much experience, it is striking to have this gifted speaker say, 'There are only three questions—"Where have I come from? Where am I going? How do I get there?".' All others revolve round these, vaguely stated at times, reaching out always into life with religious, social and political implications.

87

It was in answer to a question from the deep places of a man's being that our Lord replied: 'I am the Way, the Truth, and the Life' (John 14: 6). No one had ever spoken like that before. The Buddha, about 530 B.C. it is true, had pointed out a way to his disciples, and said, 'Walk ye in it!' But this was very different—Jesus did not merely point out a way, He said: 'I am the Way.' Here men saw no code of rules, no document, no theology, no ethical system—but a Personality. And the wonder of that is the glory of Christianity to this hour. Alice Meynell, speaking for each of us, sets it down unforgettably:

> *Thou art the Way.*
> *Hadst Thou been nothing but the goal*
> *I cannot say*
> *If Thou hadst ever met my soul.*

And to that, He adds: 'I am the Truth.' All we can claim at best is, 'We bear witness to the truth'—Jesus could claim, 'I am the Truth.' And to that, as relevantly, He can add: 'I am the Life.' Without the Way there is no going, without the Truth there is no knowing, without the Life there is no living.'

One of the loveliest tributes to a modern disciple of His must be that inscribed on the tombstone of a missionary: *Ellen Arnold walked that Way; taught that Truth; lived that Life.*

And fortunately for us, geography has nothing to do with it!

O Lord, I rejoice that Thou dost not despair of my limited powers, but dost redeem them, and fill them out with Thy divine strength and beauty. Amen.

A Pæan of Praise

WE must all be sorry to learn of the discovery of mice in the organ of Newick Church, Sussex. Mischief of some sort has been suspected for some time. In dismantling what is officially called 'the great', a nest has been found—consisting of a 1956 Chichester diocesan leaflet torn to shreds, a shoe-lace, a match-box, elastic bands from the vestry table, a toffee-paper, pieces of string, and a number of leaves from a tree in the churchyard. To an enterprising company of mice nothing comes amiss; but the net result, as far as the church is concerned, is that they have succeeded in stifling the clear notes of praise.

Praise is an essential part of worship and experience, and anything that hinders it must be counted mischievous. Praise has welled up in the hearts of men and women from the beginning of time—*the only compulsion put upon them by God, the praise-worthiness of His nature, and His acts. All true religion finds its spring here—in One possessing merit and the other moved to spontaneous recognition of it.* So we have the Psalmists raising their voices to God. They are not like the heathen round about—blindly feeling after Him if haply they might find Him—they are certain of His nearness, and of His goodness. Far from being continually on their way up to a religious festival, many are toilers like ourselves, common people, trudging at times ways difficult and drear. Still their praise finds a voice—to the glory of God, and to their own and our continual enrichment.

'Praise,' as an authority in our day, Dr Erik Routley, reminds us, 'is the foundation of all hymnody—you may say, indeed, of all singing.'

This is only the more wonderful when it rises amid discouraging circumstances. The Psalms provide many examples. And one thinks of our Lord and His little company in the Upper Room. Mark's statement is memorable, covering that night of oncoming shadows: 'And when they had sung an hymn, they went out' (Mark 14: 26). 'If,' say modern scholars, 'that Supper was the Passover, then that hymn would be the Hallel' (Psa. 115: 118). Turn it up, and you will find it filled with praise.

Centuries on—set amid a depressing little garrison town known to us as in Serbia—Nicetus presents his fellow-Christians gathered with a new song. Few can read the parchment; but together they raise the note of praise. It is, of course, the *Te Deum*, that still finds a place in our worship:

> *We praise Thee, O God;*
> *We acknowledge Thee to be the Lord.*

Circumstances, it seems, are powerless to prevent praise, if the heart is right. Padre S. J. Davies finds himself in a grim prisoner-of-war camp in North Korea, but *In Spite of Dungeons*, his account of it, tells us of his heart's song: 'O God, I praise and bless Thy wondrous Name for all Thy mercy and Thy love!'

And still nearer in our time—learning that his brief adventure here is ending, Donald Baillie, beloved Professor of Theology of St Andrews, makes one last request of his brother, Dr John, that he read the hundred and forty fifth Psalm. And what is that? A paean of praise! 'I will extol Thee, my God, O king; and I will bless Thy name for ever and ever. Every day will I bless Thee; and I will praise Thy name for ever and ever!'

What circumstances are powerless to stifle; nothing must be allowed to hinder!

O God, I praise Thee for what Thou art! In Thy hands are the issues of Life! Amen.

A Toothache

HAVE you been in Gloucester Cathedral lately? It is impossible to hush one's heart in that place of great Norman pillars, arches and other examples of craftsmen's skill, without being awed by its sheer spaciousness. But it is a pity to go there without making time to see amidst graceful carving, the figure of a little man with his face all twisted with toothache.

Who was he? It strikes us at first as humorous to see him there among the skilfully wrought symbols of the Faith. A craftsman's joke, perhaps—but a cruel joke. We don't know who he was—but we know about toothache. What had he missed, through that nagging, raging thing—a meal, Matins, Evensong? We are none of us yet far enough from childhood to forget what we sometimes missed—sweets, a bathnight, a favourite pudding, a visit.

The Russian novelist, Leonid Andreyev, has a penetrating story—though being about toothache, we stoutly refuse to call it humorous—about 'The Day of the Crucifixion'. It begins: 'On that terrible day when the universal injustice was committed, and Jesus Christ was crucified between robbers on Golgotha—on that day from early morning, Ben-Tovit, a tradesman of Jerusalem, suffered from an unendurable toothache.'

It goes on to relate how this great event appeared to a man, preoccupied with his own private woe—a trifle, in the presence of that tremendous experience. His wife tries to gain his interest, but, says the story-teller, with true insight, 'He was eager to finish the story of his toothache.'

There is no need to underline this brilliant figment of story-telling; we all too easily see ourselves in it—*missing an experience of immensity through some tremendous trifle*. It happens over and over again. Associations, friendships, human-relationships meant to lead out into wide exhilarating experiences, are spoiled before ever they have a chance to develop. Self-absorption sees to that. We are so easily caught up in a narrow world of self—our own particular pain, prejudice, point-of-view. And the glory that is part of the large purpose of God passes us by.

How often this happens in Church life; people have been known to withdraw membership, because they have not been voted to the chair of some trifling committee; to close their inward ear to truth, because of some painful little point of it that occupies their whole attention; to lose joy of service in the world Kingdom of Christ, because they cannot forget their own 'toothache'. Nobody questions its reality—but it's a small part of life, with all its rich possibilities. Self-absorption is natural enough—self-forgetfulness has to be cultivated. And it's not easy. It is a courageous Christian who prays:

> Father
> If I could only see the difference
> Between the really big and little things!
> I do not ask for better—or for more—
> I only ask for this: God keep my soul
> From growing petty.

My little self, my position, my 'toothache' is so real at times—and threatens to shut out everything else. But there is some hope of deliverance Reinhold Niebuhr believes: 'The Worship of a perfectly Holy God', he says, 'saves us from premature satisfaction with ourselves.'

O Lord, deliver me from absorption with things of self today. Amen.

Playing the Devil

WHILST I was guest in the home of my retired teacher friend, I often wondered how she managed to keep it so neat and trim always. Then one day she recited to me a poem—and I had my answer. It was called 'Ode to a Daily Help', and began:

She has her little ways,
But who has not?
For one choice virtue
Be all faults forgot,
For this let memory venerate her name,
When she promised she would come—
She came.

Just that. I would like to give you the name of that good Scottish body; but I'd better not; it might embarrass her.

But what a lovely tribute! It is six years now, since my friend recited that to me, and Mrs D . . . still comes! She grew up in the day when *to make a promise was to keep it, and to offer help was to perform it.*

One of the loveliest things ever said of a fellow-countryman of hers, was said by Pitt, of Dundas, that unobtrusive Scot: 'Dundas is no orator; he is not even a speaker—but Dundas will go out with you in any weather.' Who could ask for more?

Dependability is a quality of character all too rare in many places today. A daily-help—over the telephone—will promise all manner of things. 'Yes,' she can come, 'and the rate of pay is adequate'—but on the day set for her to begin, the chances are more than equal that she'll not turn up. A colleague in some good cause will voice his interest at the first meeting, with commendable enthusiasm—but let the

93

night of the next meeting be wet, or a set task be at some distance, and there is every chance that he will be missing. Is it true, that this is a weakness of our age, more than of any other? There are any number of employers, club-leaders, choirmasters, homemakers amongst us, to assert that it is. These, they say, are days when boys and girls, youths, and even adults refuse to be tied down. They will promise readily—and if nothing more exciting happens along at the time agreed upon, they will perform what they have promised. But one cannot be sure. So again and again life falls apart.

One thing is certain, on the authority of the New Testament, *dependability is a spiritual quality*. Blessings on those among us who know it! Paul wrote to his Christian friends in Thessalonica, a glorious thing one would like to be able to write to scores in the Church today: 'We are proud of the stedfastness and faith you display' (II Thess. 1: 4, Moffatt). Always at the back of Paul's mind, I think, echoed the accepted standard of His Lord: 'Let what you say be simply "yes" or "no"' (Matt. 5: 37, Moffatt). The New English Bible—perhaps because we need to be jolted—puts the issue even more strongly: 'Plain "Yes" or "No",' it says, 'is all you need to say: anything beyond that comes from the devil.'

I ask Thy blessing this day, O God, on all who lighten the load of others; all who serve in routine things; all who exhibit a splendid dependability. Amen.

Devotional Flowers

WHO would have dreamed that the time would come when a woman would be appointed Keeper of the Vine at Hampton Court? Yet, after twenty-six years a nursery gardener, Mary Parker has moved into 'Vine House', in the Tudor portion of the Palace, to take care of the Great Vine, planted away back in 1768. She will prune it, tend it, and at the proper season supervise the ingathering of the luscious fruit.

Change is everywhere, and this is as good an opportunity as any in which to think about it; though there are, of course, things that do not change. Our Lord spoke a great deal about vines, and nothing has happened to change the content of His words.

The daily work and economic resources of many with whom He had dealings, depended on vineyards. At Jerusalem, 'the king's vineyard,' was a well-known landmark, so that a new-comer enquiring his way, might be sent 'so many paces beyond the king's vineyard', or be instructed to 'turn left, at the king's vineyard'.

Digging a vineyard, building a tower in its midst from which to keep watch—enclosing the whole area with a stone wall to ward off robbers, and 'the little foxes which spoil the vines', pruning the branches that failed to produce healthy growth, exercising good judgement to know when and to what extent they should be cut back to the main stocks, and at last gathering in with rejoicing the luscious fruit—made up the daily work and talk of many. Some of the oldest parts of the Scriptures in which they read continually, were vintage songs: 'Saith the Lord, As the vine is found in the cluster, and one saith, Destroy it not: for a blessing is in it;

D

95

so will I do for My servants' sake, that I may not destroy them all' (Isa. 65: 8).

Those who listened to our Lord were not slow to recognize the unchanging truth in His seemingly casual references to vine growing—His talk of the labourers in the vineyard (Matt. 20: 1); His reference to the two sons—one who promised to go and work in his father's vineyard and went not, and the other who made no promise, but went (Matt. 21: 28–31); they were solemnized by His story of the man who let out his vineyard to others, and at the fruit season sent to claim what was his own, with sad results (Mark 12: 1–12); they applauded His commonsense about refusing to put new wine into old skins (Matt 9: 17); they smiled a little when He put His question, 'Do men gather grapes of thorns, or figs of thistles?' (Matt. 7: 16).

The truth of these great things remains unchanged. So, indeed, does His striking reference to Himself as the True Vine: 'I am the Vine,' and addressing His close disciples, 'ye are the branches.' Nowhere in our Christian vocabulary is a better word picture of oneness, nor a more penetrating statement of the nature of true life than in the chapter in which these words appear (John 15). Plainly, the one purpose and end of planting, digging, guarding, tending, *is fruit*—in the spirit, as in the terraced garden.

To remind us of this in our day, Evelyn Underhill chooses words well, in *The Fruits of the Spirit*: 'The spiritual life,' she says, coming straight to the point, 'consists in His action within us . . . His sap rising quietly and secretly in the soul, bringing forth, not merely nice devotional flowers—but fruits.'

O Lord, let Thy spirit dwell within me, lest I disappoint Thee. I have no human power equal to this day's possibility. Let the fruits of the Christian life be found in my work and play, in my thought and action. Amen.

Rags and Bones

I DON'T at all envy Mrs Nellie Thomas her job. Jogging along in her little cart, behind Jimmy, she is a familar figure in East Ham—London's only rag-and-bone woman. I can't tell for sure how long she has been at it. Children in the locality, I know, keep a look out for Jimmy her horse, and householders are glad of the few coins from the waste she buys from them.

She belongs, in her lowly way, to that ancient order of seekers and valuers found in bazaars and markets the world over, her chief gift that of seeing *what waste might become*.

Paul must have been familiar with such in his time. He has a colourful phrase—twice appearing in his letters: Ephesians 5: 16; Colossians 4: 5—about 'redeeming the time'. The word 'redeeming', scholars tell us, literally means 'buying out', laying hold of all that is available. It is a term which smacks of the market, and the waste merchant. One sees him—one finds it hard to think there were any Mrs Nellie Thomases in Ephesus or Colossae, though it is easy to be mistaken—threading through the streets and lanes, buying rags and bones, odd bits of metal, broken jewellery, anything that represented any worth, once it was made over.

The Greeks, it appears, had a lively sense of the value of time—as an extension of moments, and time the inert charged with opportunity, changed into purposeful activity. In using the word *kairos*, it is this latter meaning Paul has in mind. In an effort to make his injunction to the Christians of Ephesus and Colossae in Paul's day, as plain to us, Moffatt renders his words: 'make the very most of your time', and the New English Bible, 'use the present opportunity to the full.' To get the meaning of this, one has to hear it in the midst of a busy life. Bullied by modern timetables, clocks and calendars, this word comes to us with a relevancy that I can hardly imagine present in more leisurely days. But again, I could be mistaken. I know we spend a lot of time saying that there isn't time—but perhaps people have always done that. There may always have been as much need as now for this word of Paul's about *gathering up the waste bits, and turning them to some good.*

When Darwin discoursed on 'the difference between ten minutes and a quarter of an hour,' he had this sort of need in mind. 'Make careful use of the fragments of time', was how Bishop Walsham How put it. But I can't help feeling that James Barrie's old home-keeping mother, Margaret Ogilvy, touched us more closely than either scientist or bishop, when—with but ten minutes to spare before the starch was ready—she began the *Decline and Fall of the Roman Empire*, and finished the mighty work that winter!

Scraps that would be to many waste time can be to others of us the very stuff of real achievement. This is *no* argument for an earnest, hurried, distraught approach to life—far from it—it is a word on the surprising worth of waste.

You have noticed, I am sure, how much more busy people read than those who have all the time there is; how much more service in church and community is given by those who already have their professional and family-life packed, than by those who have stretches of time to themselves. Such are the real readers, the real helpers—those who have learned to 'buy up' the time.

Save me, O Lord, from wasting my time, my strength and my opportunities for adding to the sum total of life. And to Thy Name be all the glory. Amen.

Peter-Panism

A MIST blurred Kensington Gardens' outlines that early Spring day. Then suddenly I spotted beneath a small dark raincoat approaching, a chink of red. It might have gone unrecorded, save that my camera was slung over my shoulder, and before us, as we halted, in a shelter of buds, stood Peter Pan, his pipe of music uplifted. To the auntie with two children I dared my question: 'Would you allow the little girl to slip off her raincoat for a second? Peter Pan needs a little child, and some colour.'

In no time I had two charming pictures—one for my collection, one for a little girl in a red skirt, on a visit, too.

Barrie's creation of the little boy who wouldn't grow up loses none of its charm for children; but for the rest of us *Peter-Panism* is a disaster. Our Lord encouraged men and women to cultivate *childlikeness*, not *childishness*—and we dare not confuse them. 'It is never an easy business to grow up,' to use the Bishop F. R. Barry's words, 'and some people never manage it at all.'

The mark made on the garden gate, or the woodshed wall was meant to give place to another a little higher each birthday. Growth in mind is not so easily registered; and less easily still, is the most important—growth in spirit. One learns with distress that Richard Potter—father of the notable Mrs Sydney Webb—in old age, regularly repeated at nightfall his infant prayer: 'Gentle Jesus, meek and mild, look upon a little child.'

The Christian injunction is plain, none need misunderstand it: 'Go on growing in the grace and knowledge of our Lord and Saviour Jesus Christ' (II Peter 3: 18, Moffatt). There is nothing of *Peter-Panism* in it. Growth starts with life and it must continually reach up to new responsiveness. In

99

George Macdonald's novel, *Castle Warlock*, is a prayer which deserves to be lifted from the lips of a fictitious character, and used by each of us. It runs: 'Maker of me, go on making me, and let me help Thee. Come, oh Father, here I am; let us go on. I know that my words are those of a child, but it is Thy child that prays to Thee. It is Thy dark I walk in; it is Thy hand I hold.'

To do this is to grow.

And what begins here goes on. Nobody in our day understood that better than Nancy Price's old mother. Before me is a letter addressed to me by her distinguished daughter, servant of the British theatre. Her mother, she writes, liked always to think of life here as a preparatory school, as an exciting experience in growth. So her mind and spirit were both gloriously alive. 'The Bible was her familiar friend, and she was well acquainted with the old philosophers; the better to appreciate them, she started learning Greek at eighty!' Imagine it! Then follows what I shall always count one of the loveliest and most Christian comments I have come upon—one I could covet for myself: 'She filled her mind with the best to the last.'

Those who lack faith, can hardly lift their eyes beyond 'retirement', or at best, beyond 'Three-score-years-and-ten'; but here is something excitingly different. Life *Here* and Life *There* is seen to be all of a piece, and growth an essential part of it—in body, mind and spirit. Not one of us calling himself 'Christian', dare put off growing to the Life to come!

God of Truth and Beauty, give me courage to grow—to change ideas, to develop understanding, to reach out to take in more and more of Thy purpose in the world. Amen.

In the Red

I CAN'T help it: I shall always be 'in the red', though brought
up to have a horror of debt. I am not now as innocent as
Dr Nash, vicar of Leigh, though I can't forget him. I spent
a happy time in his garden-and-orchard-blessed Worcester-
shire. He used to preach once a year, I discovered, just before
the tithe audit, riding in a carriage and four from the
vicarage to the church, his favourite text: 'Owe no man
anything'.

Now that's a fine text—in its moneyed meaning—but,
apart from collecting a few tithes and clearing up a few bills,
a quite impossible one. Paul knew too much to leave it at
that: 'Owe no man anything,' he wrote, 'but to love one
another' (Rom. 13: 8). Those who received his letter knew
what he meant: he had already written to them: 'I am
debtor both to the Greeks, and to the Barbarians, both to
the wise, and to the unwise' (Rom. 1: 14). In modern
terminology, *I am in the red everywhere*.

When the Editor of the *New Yorker* writes gaily: 'At
4.20 p.m. on Wednesday June 15th, we discovered that for
the first time in our memory our affairs were in exact
financial balance: we owed nobody in the world a cent:
nobody owed us,' his lot seems at first sight a happy situation.
But, of course, it is a hopelessly unrealistic one. Except in
the limited realm of hard cash nobody is ever in that state.

Far more realistic is the statement of another modern, who
says:

> *I owe so large a debt to life,*
> *I think if I should die to-day*
> *My death would never quite repay*
> *For music, friends and careless laughter,*

The swift, light-hearted interplay
Of wit on ready wit, and after,
The silence that most blessed falls
Across the room and firelit walls . . .

Debt, one soon discovers, goes far deeper than parting up with a few paltry tithes, or posting a cheque or two. In its most real sense, it is one thing in this world that never becomes smaller when contracted. No sooner have we opened our eyes, to become part of the world family, than we are in debt. Born into a family where love is real, far more than little woollies await us—the accumulated knowledge of the race, the experience of medical science, child-care, is here; presently, storybooks, leading on to the riches of literature. A pencil and paper in a desk awaits before a trained teacher leading on to the everwidening heritage of education. And the treasures of Art and Music are ready for us. Law and order already exist for our safety and well-being, roads and pavements we are not asked to pay for await our comings and goings. Ships, trains and planes bring us food from the ends of the earth. More than any of these, there is the Christian Church, and the Scriptures, and hymns of praise.

Far from contracting, this accumulated debt—in its most real sense—grows ever greater. Though our hands be continually in our pockets, and we spend days and years in Church and Community service, we can never be 'out of the red'. This is precisely what that great modern preacher, Dr J. S. Stewart, means when he says: 'No man who is too proud to be infinitely in debt will ever be a Christian.'

O Lord, let me seek not so much to be consoled, as to console; to be understood, as to understand; to be loved, as to love. And to Thee be the glory. Amen.

Accidents will Happen

EVERY time I stand beneath Salisbury's cathedral spire, my
heart gives thanks for it. The tallest in England, it is so
graceful. No wonder artists sit for hours on their little stools
painting it, and travellers come long distances to see it.

So far as I am aware, only one man has been known to be
afraid of it. That was old William Bowles, poet and parson.
The fact that the spire had already been standing several
centuries counted nothing with him—he was afraid it would
crash on his head. To allay his fears, he took a line, and
painstakingly measured out four hundred feet across the
turf—and it came short of his house. Oddly enough when
he saw that, he felt better. Those who looked on, said with
good reason, 'Well, he's a selfish old fellow, if ever there was
one; he doesn't care what happens so long as he's safe—he
wants only to be sure that the spire won't crash down on
him.'

But we must be careful not to censure him too harshly;
people commonly had such fears at one time—believing that
if they came too near anything high, it would fall on them
for their sins. If, with time, nothing fell on them, the very
moment there was an accident of any kind, they might be
heard to exclaim: 'Well, those people must have been
sinners!' It was cruel, it was thoughtless; but something of
it still lingers, one is amazed to discover. A tall tree topples,
a tower is struck by lightning, a village is swept by a land-
slide, and we officially call it 'an act of God'.

Now all this, of course, is cruelly muddle-headed. Our
Lord had dealings with people who commonly believed
such things; and He talked to them very lovingly, but very
plainly. He reminded them of an accident over which they
had wagged their heads, and wagged their tongues—the fall

of the Tower of Siloam, with eighteen men buried beneath its dusty rubble. 'Were these men sinners above all others that this thing happened to them?' He asked. 'I tell you, No!' (Luke 13: 1-3).

And we can save ourselves and others in our day a good deal, by pausing to hear plainly the echo of His words. God is not poised above this earthly scene, ready at first opportunity, to wreak His spite upon sinners. What would such a God be? Certainly not the Father revealed to us by Jesus, from cradle to cross, and beyond.

We have to find another approach to accidents—they cannot be reckoned the revenge of God. It helps to remind ourselves—bound together as we are in the bundle of life—that unearned ill comes to us, as does unearned good. It helps further to realize that this is a world of law, where fire always burns, and water left to itself always runs down hill. If it were not so—and fire sometimes froze, and water ran up-hill—all knowledge and progress in science and life would be impossible. These things do sometimes cause accidents—the man who jumps from a height, careless or ignorant of the law of gravitation, will not break the law, *he will break his neck*. And there are other natural laws that we do not yet know.

Whatever happens, one thing is certain—on the authority of Jesus—*no accidents originate in the spite of God*. Old William Bowles should have known better.

In the quietness of this moment and in the busy demanding hours of day, O God, let my dependence on Thee, be unwavering. In health and in sickness, in safety and in accidental hurt, my hold on Thee is frail—but Thy hold of me is firm. Amen.

At the Quintain

PAST and present converged. There had been no school rule against it, when I had enlisted the aid of my parents, and together we had filled up three pages of my exercise book. A most exciting evening! I was ten, and I thought I'd never forget it; but it got overlaid with the years, until I journeyed down from London to spend a week-end with a friend in Kent. (My homework had been to find out all the words I could, beginning with 'QU'. Beginning with 'Queen'—the easiest to come to a small girl's mind—my list ended with 'quilt', as the hour for bed drew near—by way of 'quiet', and 'question'. I never dreamed there were so many. I'm not sure we didn't *invent* a few.) I know now that we left out one—the word 'quintain'. I'd never heard it till I went to Kent.

'Where shall we start?' my friend asked, the morning after my arrival. 'I know you've seen a good many of the well-known sights. Would you like to see what remains of a quintain, a mile or two from here?'

She must have guessed that I was mystified, for she set out to explain. I might have come across it myself in the dictionary, if my ten-year-old interest in 'QU' had continued, as my teacher no doubt hoped it would, and have learned that a quintain is—or was in medieval times—'a beam fixed at right angles to an upright pole and working freely on a swivel. A military pastime, often pursued against a background of crude humour. A man on horseback charged one end of the beam with his lance—causing the whole to revolve smartly, and a sandbag at the other end, to swing round and unseat him, unless he was careful.' No wonder there were guffaws. It could be serious, but when all was said and done, the unseated could have *no one to blame for the happening but himself*, however much it hurt.

No one could say that was unfair—any more than he could say it of our Lord's word about judging. 'Judge not that ye be not judged. For with what judgment we judge, ye shall be judged' (Matt. 7: 1–2). It used to puzzle me; but when Phillips' translation came out, I saw it as plain as could be: 'Don't criticize people', he says, 'and you will not be criticized.' In other words, if you suffer an uncomfortable fall, like the rider 'at the quintain', then you'd better know as clearly as he, that it's your own fault. Nobody else can be held responsible for the sandbag that has unseated you.

Now this is plain talk. Fair, of course, but plain. If Edmund Gosse had only reckoned like this, it would have taken a lot of the wicked satisfaction and sting out of the constant criticism of his fellowmen of letters. After the privilege of reading a manuscript, he would write the sweetest, most encouraging letter; and later, in company, round his own table, he would tear the wretched author to pieces. *He forgot that he was 'riding the quintain'—as a good many of us do.*

Judgement, in one sense, is the exercise of our natural power of deciding whether an action that concerns us is noble, generous, loving, or the reverse. But this is something more—scholars tell us that the Greek word is *krino*, from which we get our word criticism. Our Lord is here warning us against our readiness to judge another once and for all—as though we possessed all wisdom and authority—the judgement complete, and nothing in his favour to be said. This is dangerous. *To God alone—Who has the first word in our creation, the continuing word in our preservation—belongs the last word in judgement!*

With my own human faults, have mercy upon me that ever I have presumed to judge others, O Lord. Teach me how to forgive—even as I am forgiven. Amen.

Such a Noise

IF someone were to ask you what changes you would like to see in the world, where would you begin? Asked that question lately on the BBC, John Betjeman began with, 'Less noise,' and only then went on to other things, 'fewer cars, wider roads, more railway trains, plenty of branch lines, and a little less speed—not everything so hurried up.'

There is no doubt that noise has become a problem. In every city, every day can be heard somewhere the deafening stutter of pneumatic drills as workmen lift a piece of pavement, widen a bridge, or demolish some building standing in the way of progress. Added to this, is the thunder of wheeled traffic—noisiest of all, the modern sports-car, the adolescent-owned motor-bike—unless one counts the jet plane that rips through the sky overhead.

It is not to be wondered at that physicians and psychiatrists account a good many of our manifestations of stress to this continual noise. In some great cities I know, night noise is only a little less; its presence—even when we are not painfully conscious of it, produces extra burdens of fatigue, which shallow sleep cannot quite neutralize.

From time to time, research is focused on our problem—in the first instance to discover what kinds of noises most annoy. A thousand or so people at a time—carefully selected to be representative—are patiently questioned. Slamming doors come high up in the scale, muffled dance-music from a hall, wireless or transistor radio; after that, quarrelling adults and crying babies.

Of 2,017 people living in small or medium sized houses or flats in forty towns, the cause of annoyance divides itself into two categories—noise originating *within* their own buildings, and noise from *without*. The age and structure of the occupied buildings has naturally much to do with the problem. The close siting of buildings—to each other and to railways and main traffic-routes—is another factor. Town planners, architects and builders are all involved.

'At twenty', says one of the Royal physicians, 'we scoff at quiet; at forty we begin to think we need it; at sixty we know we cannot do without it.' The problem is not easily solved. The young in our midst are not wholly responsible for the noise we suffer. We are all to blame. The Royal physician goes on to add: 'If you will make it clear that you regard noise and fuss and needless haste as bad manners, which in effect they are, you will help us to get back the things that really make life worth living—tranquillity and beauty and power.'

In this age of wireless, transistor radios, Hi-fi recordings, electrical amplifiers, and TV, how often one is forced into business and social relationships where talk continues all through, and above, whatever programme is on. The physician is surely right—such behaviour must be counted bad manners. And perhaps it betrays another victim of the great modern phobia—fear of quiet, which is such a deep necessity of mind and heart.

This is an urgent and far reaching matter, in which we all need to accept a share of responsibility, if life is not to be strained. The saintly Janet Stuart's words come like a cool draught of commonsense: 'Think glorious thoughts of God—and serve Him with a quiet mind.'

Father, deliver me from all selfishness and clamour that make life difficult for others. Teach me consideration. And to Thy Name be the glory. Amen.

In the Maze

HAVE you been to Hampton Court lately? If you are
planning a visit, or making a return, I must tell you that
they are replanting the Maze. Something had to be done,
when it was realized that feet could be seen through gaps.
This was to give the show away. Mr Fisher, superintendent
of Hampton Court Gardens, now has the matter in hand.
In future, each border will be of a double row of yews with
an iron fence in the middle. Already a thousand little yews
have been planted. But many more will be needed, of
course, to cover the walks from end to end. And some years
must pass before the Maze—waiting on the slow ways of
Nature—can be completely replanted.

Countless youngsters, not to speak of sweethearts, and
older folk with a sense of fun, have been intrigued by it since
it was first planted away back in 1768. A remnant of a
simpler age with its geometrical style of gardening, it is still
a source of merriment. At one time, there were a number
of labyrinths planted in the gardens of great houses. Hampton Court Maze has long been considered one of the finest
in England, with its little lanes, bordered with neat clipped
hedges too high to look over, and too thick for the eye to
penetrate. The trick is to get to the centre, and then to
return. One more pretentious design belonging to the same
century, boasted 'six different entrances, whereof there is
but one that leads to the centre, and that is attended with
some difficulties and a great many stops.' That is making
fun more than fun. Most of us are content with the challenge
set us by Hampton Court Maze.

The 'know-alls' tell us how simple it is—after we've lost
ourselves—'All one has to do,' they say, 'is follow the hedge
on the *right* when going in, and the *left* when coming out.'

It sounds simple. Others make it sound more complicated: 'To reach the centre,' they say, 'go left on entering, then, on the first two occasions when there is an option, go right, but thereafter go left.'

Does anyone behave as logically as that in the Maze? Of course not. By one of those oddities of chance, on the very day this week on which I learned of the replanting of the Maze, I brought home from the Library, Norah Loft's novel of medieval life, *The Town House*. 'The Maze at Beauclaire,' I found myself reading, 'was a singular oddity.' Somebody claimed it a haunt of evil spirits, but Dame Margery soon put that to rights with her reply: 'Rubbish. It is just a puzzle, laid out in the days when people could not walk far from the castle walls for fear of enemies, so that they made the longest walk, and the most interesting on the smallest possible space.' But on the day of a cold thaw when Maude, the teller of the disaster, got lost, it was a terrifying place. At last, in the darkness, when she had given up hope, she heard a call—but an answer was beyond her powers. 'I tried,' she confessed, 'but my tongue was dry flannel between my chattering teeth.' Rescued by one with a lantern—constantly on guard—she heard him say: 'We watch. We count 'em in and we count 'em out. Come on, now follow me.' 'I don't think I was any more pious than the next,' said she ... 'Now, however, I thought—*That is like God, watching our comings and goings, Himself unseen but ready to help in time of need.*'

A sustaining discovery! I often sing:

> *Here in the maddening maze of things ...*
> *To one fixed ground my spirit clings;*
> *I know that God is good!*

O Lord, life often puzzles me; but I find strength to go on in Thy love eternal, Thy wisdom long proven, Thy patience untiring. Amen.

Priorities

AIR travel poses problems; one is allowed only so many pounds of luggage. I once worked it out so finely that I cut my cake of soap in half. The other day, a twinkle went round a group of conference delegates gathered at an airport, when a little deaconess from Germany—intent on her share of the days of thinking and planning together—turned up with a heavy bag of books. When the gaze of the group turned her way, she replied brightly, 'If these are too heavy, I'll leave my extra shoes behind.' Her shoes were heavy, it was true, and costly; and nobody wanted that. The problem was solved—but it was a nice glimpse into her priorities. What would you have done?

In these days of air travel, expeditions into frozen places, and probes into outer space, one remembers that it is just over fifty years since Shackleton set off in the *Endurance*—August 1914. By January, his little ship was well frozen into the pack-ice, hard against the western coast of the Weddell Sea. Nine months later she sank, bows first, as the ice melted. It was a desperate situation. Shackleton and his men saved what they could, and drifting, caught seals for food. They had even to kill their trusted dogs—a matter of priorities. In time, they got free of the pack-ice, and made a perilous journey towards Elephant Island.

But to do so, they had to face up to the same problem that faced the little German deaconess at the airport—the problem of priorities. What could they spare? Well, they threw away their heavy silver coins and gold sovereigns as non-essential—that wasn't so difficult, there was nowhere to spend them.

It interested me most to note what they kept—Dr Hussey's old banjo, that in days ahead might do something to keep up their spirits; and each man kept his photos and letters from home—tokens of the ties which bound them, without which life anywhere is insupportable; and they kept the title page of their Bible, given them by Queen Alexandra—and cut out others without which they couldn't live—to have kept the whole would have been too heavy. And each man, knowing well how precious it was to him, kept his spoon. What would you have kept in that situation? It is not possible, perhaps, to tell till the moment comes.

Whether you care for air travel or not, or for exploration into little-known places, you cannot be exempt from the need *to sort out priorities*.

When the wellknown author, John Gunther—was travelling in the States preparatory to writing his book, *Inside U.S.A.*, one of his 'inside' series, his number one question to officials and ordinary men and women wherever he met them, was, '*What do you believe in most?*'

In every part of life today there is a tremendous pressure on us to listen to this, to do that, to buy this, and believe that. There isn't time enough for all—we've got to sort out our priorities.

Goodspeed renders a verse of Paul's, in I Corinthians 2: 15 'The spiritual man is alive to all true values.' It's easy to say it; but is it so—have you and I got our values sorted out? It's a difficult practical issue in personal terms; more than that, it can't be settled once and for all—that is why this Christian way of life we have chosen is such a challenge.

O Lord, let me choose well this day the things that will become part of my life, colouring my imagination, moving me to action. Grant me Thy courage. Amen.

Wonder-lust

LIFE here will never be dull—of that you can be very sure. Living in this world, as we are allowed to do, everything is the stuff of wonder. Awareness begins and ends with it. The 'first wonder of the child is *ignorance*; the second is the parent of *adoration*.' Little Jamie Watt sat watching his mother's kettle boil, and the miracle of locomotion was begun; but thousands of kettles had boiled before that. 'He who can no longer wonder and stand in rapt awe,' says Einstein, one of the greatest minds of the twentieth century, 'is as good as dead—and this knowledge,' he adds, 'is at the centre of all true religiousness.'

It begins, maybe with a bath plug, or with the steam from a kitchen kettle—but it does not remain there. It meets us both indoors and out. A tree one has never truly noticed before, stands reaching upward, and one begins to wonder what it feels like to have sap suddenly rise:

> *Yesterday the twig was brown and bare;*
> *Today the glint of green is there,*
> *Tomorrow will be leaflets spare . . .*
> *I wonder what will next be there?*

All day long, such queries rise and continue into the dusk and the starry darkness. Christopher Fry, playwright of our time, made a speech at his old school a little while ago, at prize-giving. And the boys are not likely to forget it.

'If you took the next rocket to another planet,' said he, 'not, I should say, to the moon, which looks romantic enough from down here, but I believe is a rather dreary affair once you're on it—but to some other effervescent planet, where pigs flew, and flowers were likely to eat whoever was passing by, and little containers the size of your finger nail opened and let out green, gigantic living things which would never get into a house without stooping—wouldn't you be a "clot" if you weren't amazed, and raring to discover as much about the place as you could possibly get into the hours of the day? ... And yet, of course, the planet I have just most inadequately described is the one you are sitting on now, as anyone will recognize who has seen a vampire bat, or a sea anemone, or an oak tree growing out of an acorn.'

Once own that wonder is the centre of all true religiousness, and one can understand why saints like St Francis walked starry-eyed all their days; why a modern missionary counts himself one of the most fortunate on the earth to be teaching Christianity to simple tribespeople lately discovered in the New Guinea Highlands. They haven't lost a sense of wonder; everything about the Christian story is exciting to them.

So wonderful is it, that we ought all to be starry-eyed. There is scarcely anywhere a more tragic mistake than to think that knowledge drives out wonder from the world—*wonder grows with true knowledge*. The early disciples learned that the more they learned of the Risen Christ. It is recorded: 'They yet believed not for joy, and *wondered*' (Luke 24: 41).

What is the matter with us?

O Lord of Life, Thou art acquainted with all our limitations. Move us anew, this day, till for very wonder we take the shoes from off our feet. Amen.

Strangers Step in

MY sympathy goes out to the occupants of a new house at Haywards Heath, in southern England.

No question arises about the house's soundness of structure —its foundation firmly laid, its walls raised, its roof, windows and doors secured, fittings and decorations completed; but by mischance or mismanagement, it has been built over an ancient right-of-way. So the occupants have been ordered to keep their front door open day and night, to allow passers-by to enter, cross their dining room, go out, and on through the garden, into the fields beyond. A council official is trying to do something about the distressing situation; meanwhile, the law pertaining to the right-of-way persists.

Can you think of anything worse than to have strangers invade your home's privacy? 'The opening and closing of doors,' Christopher Morley rightly claims, 'are the most significant actions of our life. *'Doors,'* he adds, *'are the symbol of privacy*, of the body's retreat, of the mind's escape into blissful quietude or sad secret struggle.'

Privacy is one of our most precious rights as free persons, and anything which robs us of it, must be suspect. Countless numbers in countries today where totalitarian claims are uppermost, would give all they have for it. Nor must we forget many closer at hand in transit camps, crowded hostels, tenements, and places of temporary residence.

In subtle ways, complete strangers are likely to walk in on us. Our home need not be built over an ancient right-of-way. Men and women whom we would not think twice about inviting into our homes, stand ready to step over the threshold—through radio, and TV programmes—introducing subjects and standards unwelcome if they came in person. Equivalent to the latch on the door, is the tiny button on our respective sets. The right of entry must be clearly seen for what it is, a privilege. And the power of exclusion must be as clearly seen as the prerogative of every true home-lover.

It takes an alert mind, discrimination and some courage to preserve the precious values of the home. Especially is this important where young people, in their most impressionable years, are part of the family circle. Happily, there are enough good, glad, wholesome people ready to be invited in through these two modern mediums, to make it possible to exclude all who trade in sex, unhealthy excitement and shabby tricks. Sociability can be too dearly bought; the healthy, happy human relationships within the home are so precious. Strangers have no right to step in uninvited.

Our Lord carried this essential further when He said: 'When you pray, shut your door and pray to your Father privately' (Matt. 6: 6, Phillips). He was not ruling out acts of public worship, prayer, and friendly sharing of one's faith—not at all. He was underlining the essential value of privacy, if one is to enter, and to rejoice, in the most precious relationship of all. And His word was never more relevant.

> *A wretched thing it were to have our heart*
> *Like a broad highway or a populous street*
> *Where every idle thought has leave to meet,*
> *Pause, or pass on as in an open mart.*

O Lord of the secret places of my heart and home, I would welcome Thee anew this day. Instruct my mind, quicken my spirit, and set me to loving service. So often I have promised much, and failed—only in Thy strength is my strength. Amen.

Our Moods

'MOOD' in my dictionary leads immediately to 'Moon'—and that's how it is with lots of us. One moment finds us riding high, the next, cast down to earth as though life could never be good again.

We all have our moods. And in admitting that much, there is a temptation to claim that we know ourselves. But do we? Said a speaker on the BBC: 'I don't think anybody does . . . You may think you do, and then one day someone pops out with a little character portrait which is quite extraordinarily unlike one's picture of oneself.

'Not long ago,' she went on, 'someone suddenly said to me, "We always think of you as full of beans and jolly." "*Me*," she found herself exclaiming, "Me, like some cheery kettle hissing away on the hob? Me! Me! So drowned in despondencies and doubts and uncertainties, yet I give this person the impression of a bag of jolly jumping beans. Well, there you are."'

There is, of course, a time to laugh, and a time to weep; a time to be hopeful, a time to admit disappointment; a time to press on, a time to sit down. We were never meant to know a constant elevation of spirit.

But this is the place to point out that there is all the world of difference between *moods* and *moodiness*. Moods pass over the landscape of our souls like alternate sun and clouds over the earth. And they are as natural. Moodiness is something altogether different—a lack of control, a weakness, a loss of wholesomeness and sweetness. In *Lark Rise*, the simple ecrord of her village, Flora Thompson introduces Twister. Out in company he mixed well, ready to clown to contribute to the fun, 'But at home,' she says, 'he was morose—one of those people *who hang up their fiddle at the door when they go home,*' as the saying goes. This is moodiness.

One says—

> There are days when I go swishing
> The grasses with my cane;
> Almost wishing
> They were human and felt pain.
> There are days when I, forgetting,
> Kiss the grasses by the way;
> Half regretting
> I am man and not as they.

Moodiness, if allowed its head, can lead us to find nothing good in what we are, and nothing right in where we are. For some this is aggravated by a constitutional tendency to look always on the poor side of things. Loss of sleep, lack of exercise, a sluggish liver can work havoc. Part of our duty to God is to keep body and mind fit and fresh. But an even more important truth is that *our Faith does not depend on our feelings*—but on the unchangeable character of God. His power, His love, His mercy are above our moods. 'Why art thou cast down, O my soul?' cries the Psalmist. Then he reaches out beyond the mood of the moment to say: 'Hope thou in God' (Psa. 42: 5). And this is how the great souls of our own time deal with their moods. 'You seem to imagine that I have no ups and downs,' said Jowett of Balliol. 'By no means.' To the end of his glorious life Dr John Baillie affirmed there were things his brother Donald was unsure about—*but he was sure of God!*

And no saint—or psychologist—can share a greater secret.

Almighty God, Who creates, nourishes and gladdens all life in heaven and earth, my whole trust is in Thee. Forgive me my moodiness, my lack of faith. Amen.

Let Me be Aware

ON his way out of the lecture-hall on Wednesday night, the professor of Classics paused to enlarge for me a point he had made on awareness. He spoke of a snatch of experience passed on to him by Dr Trevor Knights.

'Employed in a bacteriological lab, it was one of his sombre tasks to identify meningitis bacteria. A positive reaction on the culture plates meant death for a child, with the unavoidable necessity of breaking the news. Once, it happened, that T.K. left some plates exposed to damp. His chief rebuked him.

'"See," he said, "mildewed—the culture is dead. We must repeat."

'As the so-called spoiled plates were dropped into the wastebin—as we know now, in the light of events—*a remedy stared at them*, twenty years before Fleming found penicillin in mildew.'

Plainly, there are things—in life, not only in a lab—that God can't give us until we are aware!

Right at the beginning, that was Jacob's story. His words revealed that, as he looked on his conscience-stricken flight from home, after a bit of shady dealing, and night found him suddenly with nothing but a stone on which to pillow his head. All that followed for him, hinged on that moment of awareness: 'Surely, the Lord is in this place' (Gen. 28: 16).

Only little by little, on up through the years—as men showed awareness—was God able to reveal more of Himself: to Isaiah His *holiness*, to Amos His *justice*, to Hosea His *mercy*.

But when, in the fullness of time, He was desirous of revealing yet more, through Jesus Christ, His Son, the awareness essential was often lacking. The New Testament

119

counterpart of that early confession of Jacob, shows through the Baptist's words, as he singles out for allegiance, the Messiah in the crowd: 'There standeth One among you Whom ye know not' (John 1: 26).

In both of these experiences—at the beginning of the Old Testament experience, and at the beginning of the New—it is easy to feel that things should have been very different. But are *we* very different? After all the centuries, with all the advantages of the revelation filled out—are we so much more aware? Hans Denk cries out: 'O my God, how does it happen in this poor old world, that Thou art so great, and yet nobody finds Thee, that Thou art so near and nobody feels Thee, that Thou givest Thyself to everybody, and nobody knows Thy name? Men flee from Thee and say they cannot find Thee; they turn their backs and say they cannot see Thee; they stop their ears, and say they cannot hear Thee.'

At the very heart of our over-all redemption, is our deep, continual need of awareness.

> *God—*
> *Grant us ears to hear,*
> *Eyes to see,*
> *Wills to obey,*
> *Hearts to love;*
> *Then declare what Thou wilt,*
> *Reveal what Thou wilt,*
> *Command what Thou wilt,*
> *Demand what Thou wilt.*

O Giver of lasting Life and Truth, quicken my awareness of Thy presence this day. Show me Thy holiness and goodness and beauty behind all common things. Amen.

Italian Stop-down

FROM time to time, student friends of mine—in transit to ancient universities—set foot in Rome. It is not easy to prepare for such an experience. I do what I can, over a cup of coffee. But plane travel means a sudden impact on one's sensibilities. One moment, the Appian Way is a picture in the back of one's Bible, the next, its tall cypresses are puncturing the sky. More ancient—and more significant to some of us, than the expected outline of St Peter's—is the pavement that carried the sandals of the saints. Together, beneath soil and gardens, some of them lie in the little-publicized Catacombs of St Priscilla. Nor can one forget the Colosseum, that great round broken-down-molar-tooth of a building. There, at the mercy of wild beasts and crowds, men and women witnessed to the Faith we hold today.

Not an inch of Rome is there, but breathes some Christian history. 'But it is a mistake to think of its witness as only in the past,' I take pleasure always in pointing out to my friends. The superintendent of the Italian Agency of the British and Foreign Bible Society, for instance—serving the same Lord—has just moved into Humility Street—Via dell'Umilta. What setting could better match one who works to such glorious purpose, or better link one with those who have witnessed from the very beginning?

The quality of Christian humility, of course, makes little *dramatic* impact. It is a word, like 'Love', 'Faith', 'Loyalty', that to our loss, has come down in our world—to some, even suggesting condescension. Though there is nothing spineless about *true* humility.

Whilst one expects to be humble before Almighty God— one is quite taken aback to find God humble before men. For this is the inner meaning of the foot washing in the

Upper Room. A servant's bowl, and the sound of tinkling water being poured into it, is part of the lasting significance of that word. How can it ever seem mean or spiritless? Surely Peter was recalling that surprising scene, his eyes misty with recollection, when he wrote in a letter—preserved now for us all—'You must put on the apron of humility to serve one another' (I Peter 5: 5, Moffatt). Plainly, he had come through a great experience. That, from Peter, of all people! (One, I think, may be forgiven for feeling that something of this Christian essential is lost in the greatness and grandeur of the basilica which bears his name aloft in Rome today—St Peter's. But there is still Via dell'Umilta —Humility Street.)

Humility is not in any sense limited to a narrow way between buildings, a mark upon the map in Rome. Not at all. Whatever printed letters fixed high on a pole by the municipality may do, to point a direction, the spirit of humility may be found as surely in a slum of Sheffield, in a school in London, a church in New York; in a home, a place of business, in a youth club. This same costly kind of witnessing that martyr Christians in early Rome knew, goes on today in many parts of the world. Paving stones break up, columns crumble, but history compounded of the spirit of the truly devoted, thank God, goes on evermore. 'God,' says Scripture, 'would not have them perfected apart from us' (Heb. 2: 40, Moffatt).

O Lord of all who travel this world's way, let me be this day so master of myself, that I may be the servant of others. In the spirit of Christ. Amen.

Always Ahead!

THE world round, there are no hills like those of little Palestine—nor wells, nor sunbaked houses, nor roads. Renan is right: 'The Holy Land is the Fifth Gospel.' Words passed over in one's New Testament reading a score of times, suddenly come alive with a new significance. Mark's words, for instance, start up out of the page: 'And they were on the road, going up to Jerusalem, and Jesus was walking ahead of them' (Mark 10: 32).

Instantly I see in that, a picture of how things were—and always will be—and not only in a physical sense. Jesus is always ahead of us. It is we who lag; He is always up-to-date. That is what a junior officer of the Oxford and Bermondsey Club tried to say, when he chose for his text, 'Two sparrows for a farthing'.

'Sparrers?' he began on a note of derision, 'We don't sell no sparrers, not in Bermondsey. *Kippers* is what 'E would 'ave said, if 'E'd been 'ere. A pair of Kippers sold for three-'aipence—*that's* wot 'E meant.'

In a few more sentences, 'sharp enough to catch that moment's insight', he compared the worth of the least of club members with even the best of kippers, and a dark corner of the Gospel was immediately flooded with a bright light.

Dusty feet still tread roads up to Jerusalem—but there are cars and jeeps, too; and you may be sure He would mention them if He were giving His teaching today. He was always ahead. A cup of cold water can still be one of life's good gifts to a neighbour—but so can a cup of coffee. And He wouldn't overlook that. A donkey can still bring one across the border; but so can a plane, as I know full well. He dealt with people as they were, where they were—every

123

word He spoke, every story He told, shot through with a lively relevance. Sparrows? Yes—because the people to whom He spoke, saw them daily, 'two for a farthing', 'five for two farthings', plucked and skewered, in the market-place, food of the poor. Cold water? Yes—in that climate, one cup given in His name might spell the difference between life and death.

> *He spoke of lilies, wine and corn,*
> *The sparrow and the raven;*
> *And words so natural, yet so wise,*
> *Were on men's hearts engraven . . .*

One moment they felt Him close beside them—the next, they knew He was away out ahead. And the wisest and most thoughtful among us today know it still. The trouble with our confused modern world is not that the teaching of Jesus about God, the sanctity of life, and our relationships with our fellows, and final destiny is out-of-date, but that *we haven't caught up with Him*. Were He speaking to men and women today in the midst of life, as in the days of His flesh, He might well set His message in our modern idiom—exchanging sparrows for kippers, cold water for coffee, patient donkeys for jeeps, speaking in turn, of jets, atoms, capsules, and all the rest; but of this fact there need be no question—nothing need be done about *the content of that teaching*. An irrelevant gospel is no gospel at all—none knew that better than He—and a modern Christian speaks with startling insight, when he says: '*Son of Man . . . Thou art abreast of all the centuries. I never come up to Thee, modern as I am.*'

He is always well out ahead!

O Lord, I bring Thee my praise and adoration. I rejoice that the whole of my life is of importance to Thee. I rejoice that no gift or discovery that ministers to Thy ongoing purpose is negligible. Amen.

By the Jordan

I was not dreaming; but it was one of those moments when I had to pinch myself to be sure I was fully awake. At that early hour the day's heat was not as great as it would be later. The slow, placid river took a bend near the place of the Baptism. It might have been any one of a dozen rivers I know—the Evenlode, the Avon, tree-shaded in Warwickshire meadows, or the one I knew earliest in life at the end of our farm. Only here were tamarisk trees to mark its way, and afford a little shade.

No one at this date, could say with certainty that this was the exact spot where Jesus stepped down into the waters before John the Baptist; but it was the site hallowed by countless pilgrims, and established by tradition from the sixth century. A few yards one way or the other, seemed to me hardly to matter—in this modest river, in this country, in Time, this great thing happened. And hereabouts, the confident, far-reaching voice of John the Baptist was heard: 'Repent ye: for the kingdom of heaven is at hand!' (Matt. 3: 2).

No sound stirred the air, as remembering these events, I stood there; least of all that shocking word of John: 'Repent ye!' It's a word we seldom hear these days—I might almost say, never. It is what someone had called a 'Janus word'—from the name of one of the oldest Latin gods, with two heads, one looking each way, considering the past, and looking to the future. John, we are told, did no miracle, but to the crowds beside this little river, he thundered out his call. And he knew what he meant by it—a grief for past unworthiness, and a readiness to make a new beginning. It involved a deliberate act of will—nothing less.

It presupposed that those who heard it were in a sinful

state. But it was not only John the Forerunner's private and particular call, reverberating there beside the gentle Jordan. The Gospel record makes that clear (Mark 1: 14–15). After Jesus had stepped down into the waters of Baptism, had known the approving word of God, 'Thou art my beloved Son, in whom I am well pleased,' and had returned from His forty days in the Wilderness, and was Himself preaching —albeit, with gentler tones than those of John, we like to tell ourselves, though this may be self-deception—the challenge was taken up again: 'Now after that John was put in prison, Jesus came into Galilee, preaching . . . saying, The time is fulfilled, and the kingdom of God is at hand, repent ye!'

But this challenge did not peter out with John the Baptist, nor with our Lord; it has its central place in the preaching of the first disciples, sent out two by two. Of them we read: 'They went out, and preached that men should repent' (Mark 6: 7–12).

It seems to me—or am I mistaken?—that this 'Janus word' ought still to be central in our preaching 'This is a harsh word for us,' said Bishop Gerald Kennedy, of the Los Angeles Area, Methodist Church, who paid us a visit lately, 'and we have taken it out of our modern vocabulary almost completely. An American does not want to repent, but desires to change the income tax laws or search for an economic panacea. The Church does not want to repent, but desires to try a new programme or organize a new committee. Persons do not want to repent, but think there must be some prescription for happiness that they have overlooked and that can be obtained without too much bother.'

But are we different from the first crowd beside the Jordan?

O God, forgive me if I have been slow to repent; if I have been eager for the punishment of any; if I have myself been wanting in mercy and love. Amen.

Awkward Question

SEVEN simple words are associated in my mind with the privilege of serving on a certain committee. Before it young men present themselves as candidates for the Christian ministry. Questions are asked on that joyous, solemn occasion—well-tried questions to test a man's call, the soundness of his faith, his education, and experience in leadership. But there is always one more question that I'd like asked, that is never asked: '*What have they seen in thine house?*' The words are Isaiah's, addressed to a king; but they have a biting penetration unmatched by any other seven words I can think of today.

Whatever the answers to those other questions, I feel a great deal hinges on the answer forthcoming to this one: 'What have they seen in thine house?'—of Christian witness, of temper, of tolerance, of thought for others? There will be college principals, works managers, and ministers ready to speak up for those known to them who come to this crossroads of choice. But is their word enough? Not to my mind.

I would put these words not only to candidates for the Christian ministry, but to every lay preacher setting out, every youth club leader, every official of the Women's Guild, of the Men's Club, to every member of the Communicants' Class, indeed, to everyone in Church Membership: 'What have they seen in thine house?'—'they' meaning, the tradespeople, the neighbours, the relations, the family.

In one of John Galsworthy's books, there is reported the answer to young Jolyn's question to his father: 'Do you believe in God, Dad: I've never really known?' The head of the house is introduced sympathetically; but surely a son who had shared the same house for years ought not to have to ask such a question. He ought to know, along with every other living soul in the house, whether he is a man of Christian faith, or not.

Once, a father took his stand on Christian things early in the day, at family prayers. That was in the time when children were raised on porridge and the Bible—now, some say, they are raised on 'corn-flakes and comic-strips'. I don't know. But the young Jolyns in our homes, ought not to be left in any doubt about where we stand in Christian values.

Bricks-and-mortar, balanced diets, TV, and wall-to-wall carpets are not enough. Things are important. But home is more even than a place to run to with chickenpox, or when the world has blackened one's eye, or bruised one's sensibilities—it's where one's earliest and most lasting of life's securities are established.

'There is nothing better than this,' said a poet centuries ago, 'when a man and woman, sharing the same ideas about life, keep home together. It is a thing which causes pain to their enemies and pleasure to their friends. But only they themselves know what it really means.'

In the deepest, personal sense, yes; but in a very real, far-reaching sense, this is not so. Every young Jolyn has a pretty good idea whether religion is a vague thing with Father, or a vital, life-giving experience. To be married but miserable is no witness; to be a Bible reader but a bickerer is no witness; to be universally admired but undisciplined at home is to fail.

'What have they seen in thine house?' *Awkward question? I agree; but there's no escaping it.*

Grant, O God, that my tongue which has sung Thy praise in public, may be saved from untruth, clamour and dispute at home; that my witness may be whole-hearted and firm. Amen.

Happy, But . . .

OBLONG is still my favourite shape for a gift-parcel, though I am continually astonished at how differently people approach a new book. Some turn immediately to the last page to 'see if she got him in the end', or, on a less amorous level, 'to learn what the hero died of '.

I am not tempted to this short-cut. I doubt whether it is ever possible to know the end, till one has shared the earlier experience, beginning at the beginning, and in time arriving at the end. Certainly that way a rich ending seems doubly rich.

I have just laid down Peter Scott's autobiography—artist, ornithologist, adventurer in three elements, land, sea and air, lecturer, founder and director of the Wildfowl Trust. In his last paragraph—after 662 zestful pages—I find him saying: 'As I contemplate all these things, I am more than ever convinced that I am the luckiest man I know. I say this not with smugness or self-satisfaction, but because I can think of nothing sadder than to live a happy life without recognizing it.'

It is possible? Peter Scott thinks so. Happiness is not easy to define, amidst first eager undertakings, the exacting experiences of middle-years, the sum total of sorrows and frustrations. Though it is something we all seek. Do any of us, in actual fact, 'live a happy life without recognizing it'?

Admiral Peary's quest for the North Pole intrigued me from the moment I heard about it. Twelve long years he spent in the Arctic. On his eighth expedition he actually found what he was seeking; but not easily. Overhead were thick clouds always as he slogged through ice and snow. Only when the sun at last broke through, and he could use his instruments, did he find that he had reached the Pole, on April 1st, 1909—*and walked right past it!* Retracing his steps eight miles, he missed it again; and four times he crossed that way, till he knew without doubt that he had found what he sought.

Is Peter Scott—son of another great explorer—suggesting that we do that with happiness? Are we inclined to value too lightly the age into which we are born, and the national setting—imagining ourselves happier in nomadic times, in the days of the Tudors, the Victorians? Being who we are, set down where we are, with particular present-day characteristics and skills, is it possible to look too far ahead? 'When we get out of this house,' we say, 'we'll be happy,' or 'When we get a rise in salary,' or 'the children are through their schooling,' or 'When we're free to travel.'

But why not now? And where this task finds us? As Christians, maybe we ought to make time to sit quietly for a few moments and think about this. Eternal Life, with all that it holds of reality and happiness, is not to be had only in the great future. 'Tis here and now! Our Lord's story of 'the two lost sons', suddenly seems real. For, of course, there were *two*—one off on a spending spree that ended painfully at the swine troughs of the far country; the other, the stay-at-home, more nearly typifying us, maybe—the happily-positioned, *but unmindful of it.* Not to the prodigal, but to this son were the words of the great Father addressed: 'Son, thou art ever with me, and all that I have is thine!'

But do we recognize our attitude?

O God, my Father, Thou hast made me Thy child! Stab my spirit broad awake this day that I may rejoice in this glorious relationship, and live. Amen.

Wide Margins

TODAY I came across a charming marginal note by a scribe of the 9th century. He was Irish. 'Pleasant to me,' he wrote, little dreaming that anyone would be considering his words all these centuries later, 'is the glittering of the sun today upon these margins because it flickers so.'

He has gone upon his way, but the blessed sun that he rejoiced in is with us still—so are his margins. We need them.

Many of us nowadays are too busy making a living to have time to live. We rush hither and thither. We have contrived by the use of modern transport and gadgets, to 'fill the unforgiving minute with sixty second's worth of distance run'; but what have we got for it? A fuller bank-book, a duodenal ulcer, a near nervous-breakdown. We have forgotten the margins.

My friend, Dr Frank Boreham, says very strikingly: 'A good life, like a good book, should have a good margin.' He adds: 'I hate books whose pages are so crowded that you cannot handle them without putting your thumbs on the type. And, in exactly the same way, there are very few things more repelling than the feeling that a man has no time for you. It may be an excellent book; but if it has no margin, I shall never grow fond of it. He may be an excellent man; but if he lacks leisure, restfulness, poise, I shall never be able to love him. The man may get through an amazing amount of work, but,' concludes my friend, 'he would be much better off in the long run if he cultivated a margin.'

Few of us are obliged to work the long hours that our fathers and mothers knew, not to speak of our grandfathers and grandmothers. Yet life for many of us out of working hours is also a feverish rush—social engagements lacking leisured reflection, recreation highly specialized and meticulously organized. Days and nights filled with activity, can give us some things—but not enough. To worship, to wonder, to know the liberating power of imagination, to read, to think, to cultivate friendship at any worthwhile level, takes time.

Few of us, of course, in this age can expect to escape the fretful demands of life as did Thoreau, and take ourselves off to the modern equivalent of the woods of Walden; we've got to work out our philosophy where we are. Nevertheless, we have to give him credit for a glimpse of essential good sense. 'I did not even read books the first summer,' said he, 'I hoed beans. Nay, I often did better than this. There were times when I could not afford to sacrifice the bloom of the present moment to any work, whether of the head or hands. I love a broad margin to my life.'

The reduction of our compulsory working hours is a wonderful advantage; but what are we doing with our leisure? Most of us work eight hours a day—a third of our lives—remaining free to plan for the rest. But a flabby mind, like a flabby body is excluded from so many of life's finest experiences. Devitalized leisure is as big a waste as devitalized labour. The late Dr T. W. Manson of Manchester University strikes a thoroughly modern and useful note for us in our philosophy of the margin, when he says: 'One of the fundamentals of education is to teach people how to use their spare time and their spare money.' A wide margin means so much!

I bless Thee, O God, for the delights of leisure. Let me keep at a distance this day, all that would spoil freshness, fitness and service. Amen.

Sure of the Morning

I DON'T always read in full the 'Births, Deaths and Marriages' in the daily-paper—being satisfied to run my eyes down the column of surnames in heavy type. A familiar name pulls me up at once; and sometimes sends me on my way with a larger understanding of this earth's brief adventure. I found the death notice of one of our ministers doing that for me. Set out unforgettably, it read: 'Greenwood, Rev. Fred.' Then the date: 'at Wesley Haven, dearly loved friend of Agnes, Freda and Ivor Skinner. *Only goodnight.*'

It was the last two words that sent me on my way enriched—so simple they were, and so profoundly Christian. To say 'Goodnight' in that calm way at the end of life's day, is only possible to those who are sure of the '*morning*'.

Thomas Guthrie, one of Scotland's great preachers and philanthropists, asked that this splendid assurance should be inscribed on his stone. And those who laid his body in the Grange Cemetery in Edinburgh, were mindful of his simple request. He wanted no grandiloquent epitaph—only some words from Amos, that might arrest the passerby: 'Seek Him . . . that turneth the shadow of Death into the morning!' (Amos 5: 8). And where in all this world could one find more striking words? Of course, we read them now in the light of the Resurrection of our Lord.

Dr Goodspeed, in his New Testament, has translated the word 'Hail!' the first word spoken by our Risen Lord as 'Good Morning!' In so doing, he has added significance to this familar phrase of our daily life, and new hope to our hearts. For our experience of Death, and what lies beyond, depends on Him. 'If Christ be *not* risen, then is our preaching vain, and your faith is also vain' (I Cor. 15: 14). But Christ *is*

133

risen! Nothing in His claim is better substantiated. Even those who once found faith difficult, were won over—men and women of the build of Thomas, for whom the unexpected spelt disbelief.

All down the long years, men and women have faced what life has brought, in the splendid confidence that all weariness, frustration and failure that can be theirs, is linked with an eternal 'morning'. So the beloved, saintly Dr F. B. Meyer wrote: 'Dear— I have just heard to my surprise that I have only a few more days to live . . . Don't trouble to write—we shall meet in the morning.'

Finding the years mounting, it was this same faith which led Dr John G. Paton to write: 'My hope for the evening of life is the hope of life's morning.'

One of the most widely-loved young ministers of our day was Dr Peter Marshall of Washington. In his biography, *A Man Called Peter*, his wife tells how he was carried from his house to the hospital on a stretcher. In this unexpected happening, he turned to his wife, and said casually: 'I'll see you in the morning.' That night he died. Those simple words have now rightly enough become the parting witness he was able to bear to that great togetherness of the Here and There. And those who had to let him go, found themselves girded about with a glorious hope. In very truth, they believed they would see him in the morning!

And every Christian has this faith!

O Lord, I bring Thee my wondering thanks for my life here in Time—and my life beyond Time. Let the reality of Thy Resurrection colour all my days, and teach me the difference between true values and those of little worth. Amen.

A Poor Stopping-place

HAVE the words that Thomas Hardy wrote across the opening page of his play, *The Dynasts*, ever struck you? 'Intended for mental performance only.' He set them there deliberately, of course.

But 'mental performance only' will not do for family life, community involvement or religion.

That is not to say that each might not be greatly benefited by a little more mental performance; but that is a poor stopping place. To take family life first, with its early lessons and emotional pressures, its ever changing circumstances and establishment of priorities; scarcely anything here remains static, as in the family portrait neatly mounted for the pleasure of the relations. The plans of yesterday, the theories picked up from the best family guidance books, the shared experiences of friends in the same age group, all have to go beyond 'mental performance.'

The same applies to community involvement—just outside that first circle of intimate relationships—the needy tangle of others' lives. Morning by morning, newspaper-headlines remind us of it; the books we read, the radio and TV programmes we share, bring us the mixed stuff of which it is made, and lay it down on the doorstep of our minds. We have to give it thought; but we fail as persons if we make that our stopping place.

And a like challenge confronts us in our religious life. The liberating truth still stands: 'God hath not given us the spirit of fear; but of power, and of love, and of a sound mind.' Unhappily, many church folk who would be deeply ashamed of ignorance in matters of family and community, are not in the least perturbed to be ignoramuses in things of religion. A few half-remembered scraps of Sunday School lessons, a few partly digested sermons from chapel-going at boarding-school, a mass of prejudices picked up from business and wider contacts in the bustling world, make up their spiritual stock-in-trade. One could wish for them a real measure of 'mental performance'—endless activity, replaced by some honest thought.

Dr Glover's words to those of us who write and speak have today an even greater relevance than when he spoke them: 'If we are effectively to preach Christ, we must secure that He is not in the minds of thinking people associated with antiquated scholarship or discredited science.' All round, the continual challenge is to serve the Lord our God with our minds, as well as our emotions. Just as there are some things which He cannot do in the world until we love, there are some things He cannot do until we think.

But religion, if it is to be rich and whole, cannot stop there—we dare not write across it the words Hardy wrote across his play—it is never for 'mental performance only'. That was the charge against the priest and levite on the Jerusalem-Jericho road. More than shining truth of the mind, and high emotion of the heart, there must be deeds of a Christlike kind. 'If ye know these things,' said Jesus speaking to His disciples of the things that stand central, 'happy are ye if ye do them.' Cloistered thought, church services and study groups are not an end in themselves. Lord Birkett, the distinguished modern judge, liked to say that his favourite epitaph was a line from the same Thomas Hardy: 'You was a good man and did good things.'

Almighty God, let me meet with eagerness this day, every opportunity for service. Let the thoughts of my mind, and the skills of my hands unite. Amen.

On the Wall

I TURNED into Wellington Street again this morning—the second time in weeks. I am not often in that part of the city. The sound of wrenching nails and rending timbers reached my ears—painfully declaring that the hour had come.

Where men and women through the generations had hushed their hearts in the presence of the Eternal, now workmen sweated with crow-bars; where countless sincere prayers had ascended, now rose clouds of dust. For some time the old church of St James' had been marked for demolition. In my private pilgrimage to one of its quiet pews, and on through to its preachers' vestry, a week or so earlier, I had only just been in time—today, I realized, would have been too late.

I wanted to satisfy myself about an inscription on its vestry wall. Was it still there? Over the years I had heard from one guest preacher after another, what its penetrating message had meant to him. The incomparable Denny—the beloved Doctor, and Principal of the Free Church of Scotland—had uttered it first: but in its simplicity, it was ageless: 'No man can at one and the same time convey the impression that he himself is clever and that Christ is mighty to save.'

In the quiet moments of waiting before the vestry door opens on the way to the pulpit, I can think of nothing that might more tellingly confront a preacher. A man called to declare the truth of God, in a public place, does not *automatically* become less self-conscious, less subject to temptation.

If it seems to those of us who sit in the pew that the subtle temptations that bedevil us are utterly unknown to those called to preach, it is time we thought through the whole situation again, and more sympathetically. As far back as

1656, John Evelyn, in his famous 'Diary' made reference to a preacher who 'made a confused discourse with a great deale of Greeke and ostentation of learning to but little purpose.' And he can't have been alone in that; for in that same century Bishop Jeremy Taylor, in his widely read *Holy Living and Holy Dying*, detailed fourteen 'Means and Exercises of obtaining and increasing the Grace of Humility' —and they were not all for Christians in the pew. Said saintly Richard Baxter: 'The most reverent preacher that speaks as if he saw the face of God, doth more affect my heart, though with common words, than an unreverent man with most exquisite preparation.'

And from that century to this, there has never been the least doubt about it. In our own day—temptations having changed so little—the beloved Dr Halford Luccock, twenty-five years Professor of Homiletics at Yale Divinity School, takes his courage in both hands to say: 'When the passion for display lays hold of a person, it gets in the way of other and better qualities. We see it at work in the reported confidential remark of a preacher to a friend. "I preached a powerful sermon on humility." He preached it. Too bad he didn't hear it!' Pride is so insidious.

Learning, gifts of utterance, success—all these and as many others, have to be battled with in the secret place, if we are to become preachers effective in the pulpit. Ministers or laity, it makes no difference: 'No man—or woman—can at one and the same time convey the impression that he, she is clever, and that Christ is mighty to save.'

Almighty God, deliver me this day from subtle forms of self-praise. Amen.

Wool-gathering

As a twin—never required to manage with one top-coat, one school-book between two—I was greatly surprised to find that apparently there weren't enough *words to go round, and that some had to do service twice*. A 'cap' could cover a knee or be a covering for a playmate's head; 'cricket' could be the name of a lively exciting insect in the grass or a game. On Saturdays one could go 'wool-gathering' along the barbed-wire fences and barberry-hedges, picking off the pieces that lodged where sheep had grazed too close, or had pushed through to succulent green just out of bounds. It brought a little pocket-money—but also a problem.

For it wasn't long before my father found me looking into space, my homework still unfinished.

'What, *wool-gathering* again!' he would comment.

What made it more difficult for me was that it wasn't Saturday when he said it, and I wasn't out-of-doors. I heard it many a time in my growing up; and somehow got it sorted out.

Less and less since have I found myself charged with 'wool-gathering'—which is how it should be; but that is not to say that it has ceased to be a problem. Life isn't so simple. In maturity 'wool-gathering' has taken on other forms, that's all.

One of the areas in which it continues, is in one's private devotions. And I have found that I am by no means alone in this. Everyday interests press in so early on waking—children's voices, street sounds, distracting thoughts, decisions tied to tasks unfinished, or to responsibilities of the wakening day.

'Nothing makes one more conscious of poverty and shallowness,' admits Jowett of Balliol, 'than difficulty in praying or attending to prayer. Any thoughts about self, thoughts of evil, day dreams, love fancies easily find an abode in the mind. But the thoughts of God, and of right, and truth will not stay there ... For two minutes I cannot keep my mind upon them.' To find such a Christian owning to something so human is an encouragement.

Looking back over countless speaking engagements, the privilege of addressing a company that filled Wellington Church, Glasgow, with some hundreds overflowing into an adjacent hall, is likely to remain a fresh memory. On that occasion, I was moved to find myself actually standing in the pulpit from which Dr George Morrison had ministered. One of my heroes—thanks to his published sermons, his biography, and the many things those privileged to sit under him have told me—part of the real debt I owe him, is for the measure of encouragement and help following on his confession of 'wool-gathering'. In his early ministry, his mind was often vagrant and unheeding; and the moment came when he felt driven to do something about it. He determined not to get up from his knees till he had not merely repeated the Lord's Prayer, but had really *prayed* it through. Ten times—beginning with the all-too-familar words—he found his mind at some stage 'wool-gathering', and only at the *eleventh* attempt did he really pray it through, entering into its rich content.

After that, I shall be longer reaching the point at which I feel I must give up. If a modern saint of his stature can confess to as much, make a new pattern of approach, and persevere till the habit yields to reality, no one need despair.

I would hush my heart, O Lord, that Thy good will may be known to me. So many things creep in to distract me. My heart is wayward, and full of fault. Forgive me my 'wool-gathering', and grant me strength to be more receptive. Amen.

A New Year Letter

HAS the 'postie' been yet? On the first day of January 1797, Horatio Nelson, a captain on a ship in the Mediterranean, wrote to his father: 'My dear father, on this day I am certain you will send me a letter.'

At the turn of another year, his words are a reminder of the affection and encouragement a letter can convey. It need not be long, it need not carry world shattering news—just to be remembered means so much. The mere sight of familiar handwriting on the envelope lifts one's spirit. One of the happiest times of any day for me—let alone the first of January—is when the mail comes at morning-coffee time.

A letter can cross continents, and make the world contract, as easily as it can hasten from the next suburb, or bring a hint of green growing things from the country. 'It really is a heavenly gift,' as Katherine Mansfield writes refreshingly, 'to be able to put yourself, jasmine, summer grass, a king-fisher, a poet, a pony, an excursion, the new sponge-bag and bedroom-slippers into an envelope.' The best letters are of this kind—right out of life, into life. Some are witty, some wise, some tender, a few indiscreet, but all are unstudied and utterly human.

Business letters are another matter altogether—dictated, self-consciously phrased, typed, beginning 'Dear Sir', 'Dear Madam'. One cannot escape these in an orderly life; but it is of the more personal kind I am thinking. They are not meant to be filed for further reference, any more than they are meant to be literature—though some, with the passing of time, have actually found their way into permanent records. Among the most treasured volumes on my shelves are such—beginning with the Paston letters, written and received away back between 1434–1509. Full of simple charm, they mirror as nothing else, daily joys, moods and domestic concerns. 'Be this delivered in haste, in right good haste,' is inscribed across one, for the benefit of the bearer; for the delivery of a letter of any sort in those times was a major undertaking. Those that have survived, retain their charm because of their naturalness—being letters about some particular matter, written with no great consideration of style, usually for one pair of eyes only. Since, other collections have been made—letters of Cowper, of Keats, and in our day, letters of Temple Gairdner, of Winifred Holtby, of Rose Macaulay—all of which I value.

But those which mean most to me will never get into print. And those which you will write and send on their way at the beginning of the year, will not depend upon such permanence for their worth either.

The telephone, the telegram, the hurry and scurry in our complex modern life have a lot to answer for, in warm human relations. One of the first to be affected is the simple practice of letter writing. And it's a thousand pities. Apart from the fact that historians of the future are going to be poorer for lack of these personal touches, spelling out the character of a century better than anything else, a relationship of lasting value is in danger of being lost. Nothing makes up for a good letter.

It is true, people in the old days, when letter writing was at its height, did have more time, but that excuse mustn't be allowed to rob us of something we can ill spare. If we have grown casual, is there any time better than New Year in which to make a new start?

O Lord, Thy purpose for us is life—life more abundant. Enrich our sense of Thy nearness by every means possible—and our awareness of our fellows. Amen.

Angry, Are You?

A BELL is rung and a story told in Wroclaw—the old thriving city on the Oder, till partly destroyed in defence by Russian artillery and handed over to the republic of Poland. Cast over five hundred years ago, the bell goes by the name of 'the poor sinner's bell'.

When all was in readiness for its casting, the story goes, the founder absented himself for a few minutes, leaving a boy in charge of the furnace. Warned not to meddle, he became fascinated by the catch which secured the seething metal in the cauldron. He took hold of it and to his terror, metal began flowing into the mould. He called for help, and the bell founder came rushing in. Madly angry to see spoiled what he hoped would be his masterpiece, he slew the boy on the spot. Only later—the metal cooled, mould opened, and his bell found to be well nigh perfect—did he come to his senses. Realizing the heinousness of his anger, he at once gave himself up. And condemned, he went to his death; whilst his bell rang out an appeal to all to pray for the poor sinner.

His bell is well-named 'the poor sinner's bell'.

Through its terrible undertones, it is difficult to remember that one can know anger *without* sin. Yet this is the truth. 'Be ye angry, and sin not,' is how Paul puts it, and it is scarcely possible to improve on that terse statement (Eph. 4: 26). Commenting upon it, Dr William Barclay, always so lucid, at first surprises us. He says: 'Anger is one of God's greatest gifts to men. But anger,' he adds, sensing that this will be difficult for many a one among us to understand, 'is like a strong medicine, which if it is used in the right way, can do infinite good, and which, if used in the wrong way, can do infinite harm. What, then, is the rule for anger? *When anger is for our own sake, it is always wrong. When anger is for the sake of others, it is often divinely right.'*

Half a moment's reflection on the record of those who have left their mark on our life will confirm this. One thinks of Shaftesbury's anger at sight of tiny children set to work above their powers; of Samuel Plimsoll's anger when apathy met his concern for countless men lost at sea in overloaded ships, and his long battle for a compulsory load-line, that today we have marked on all our merchant ships—the Plimsoll line.

Nor have there been lacking women with 'righteous anger'. Catherine Booth is only one of modern times—following on with the great task of resistence to evil, which makes anger shine with a Christlike quality; another was Emma Cons, aunt of Dame Lilian Baylis of the Old Vic Theatre—in her anger at the evil of gin taverns—providing regular rent collections, coffee taverns, and good wholesome entertainment. In this sense, *a Christian without anger is only half a Christian.*

But what most of us have to watch is 'sinful anger' that springs so easily from immediate selfish concern. I drove into the city tonight—only to be stopped at the junction of a new highway, by a board with the words DANGER ROAD UP. I reduced speed, to stop, and in the split second necessary to take in the situation, saw that some wit, or halfwit, had crossed out the first letter—so the warning read ANGER ROAD UP!

Where there is anger of the sinful kind, *the road is always up:* there is no communication between God and man, and man and man!

O Lord, let my contribution to life this day, be of a positive quality. Amen.

A Curse

CASUALNESS curses us all. But my eyes brightened as the mail brought me a letter bearing a new stamp—for the first time featuring an individual alongside the Queen. My surprise was exactly what the Post Office had intended, of course. And through the mail have now come lavishly illustrated magazines, reminding me of a happy stay in Stratford-on-Avon, and closer still, of my records of Dame Edith Evans reading the Bard's Sonnets. And my ears have quickened to specially prepared broadcasts.

After all, four-hundred years is a long time, and it is good to stab us out of our casualness. A rich heritage can so easily suffer.

For some time now, I have been looking afresh at a little picture—eight inches by seven—on our lounge wall. Painted on hammered metal, the features of William Shakespeare look out from a dark background. I like it. Nobody knows now who painted it, or how it came into our possession. I took it once to Sotheby's, the world-famous art centre, when I was going to London. Somebody said it might be valuable. (I hasten to add, it isn't.)

One of the amazements of that great centre, is how many things accepted casually, are found to be of great worth. A little while ago, an expert went to a suburban home where a member of a family was packing up her father's things. A local dealer was already on the spot, offering a meagre sum for one or two articles of his choice.

'But you've got some marvellous stuff here,' said Sotheby's man, 'those vases for example.'

'Nonsense,' retorted the local dealer, 'not worth more than a fiver.'

'Worth more than £2,000,' insisted the man from Sotheby's.

Subsequently the pair was sold for £3,800. And it keeps on happening in this casual world!

This is reason enough for a Shakespeare celebration—with stamps, literary articles and broadcasts—and the time I have lately spent before that little picture on our wall. And it is reason enough surely for considering for a moment how wide-spread is this curse of casualness in other areas of our life. 'The things which are seen are transient,' says Paul, 'but the things which are unseen are eternal' (II Cor. 4: 18). The truth of this so seldom reaches us where we are in any down-to-earth fashion. It seems a little remote.

But eternal values are not only to do with the world to which we go, at the end of this earthly adventure—they are for here and now.

We are so casual. We hear of these things from the pulpit, we read of them—and there the matter ends. One of Thornton Wilder's characters, in *Our Town*—after pondering on his own experience—comes out with words that set down this great positive truth that Paul cared so much about, in terms that the simplest can understand: 'I don't care what they say with their mouths, everybody knows that *something* is eternal. And it ain't houses, and it ain't names, and it ain't earth, and it ain't even the stars . . . Everybody knows in his bones,' says he, struggling for the right words, 'that something is eternal, and *that* something has to do with human beings.' Then he adds, thoroughly puzzled, 'All the greatest people who ever lived have been telling us that . . . *and yet you'd be surprised how people are always losing hold of it.'*

Casualness—that's our curse!

Everliving, seeking God, Who comes to me along unexpected paths, save me from carelessness and casualness. Quicken my awareness of Thee in the affairs of this day. Amen.

Stand on It

Ruth Draper's death was a great loss to those who saw her often—not less to those of us who saw her once or twice, and hoped to do so again. I have her monologues printed from the manuscript somebody persuaded her to set down just in time, together with the memoir and prefatory note by her friend, Dr Morton Dauwen Zabel, Professor at the University of Chicago. Thirty pages of delightful portraits are in the book—as child, schoolgirl, solo-stage personality, as Honorary Doctor of Law of the University of Edinburgh, later as Commander of the British Empire, later again, as Honorary Doctor of Law of Cambridge University, and in living delineations of varied characters she so tellingly portrayed. But nothing makes up for those inimitable presentations—all alone, with the flick of a shawl, or some piece of property as simple, peopling a stage with groups and crowds. Sensitive, humorous, strong, we know we shall not meet her like again for many a day, if ever.

Leafing through the volume in a moment of leisure, I came upon a letter addressed to her by Henry James, and a delightful word addressed to her in person, as she talked over her dreams at thirty—having proved her gift, and given pleasure to many private audiences. Should she listen to her friends and attempt a wider yet professional career or turn to something else? In an inspired moment, with wonder and deliberate speech, James gave her just the push she needed. '*My dear child ... you ... have woven ... your own ... very beautiful ... little Persian carpet ... Stand on it!*'

And that is exactly what she did.

Would to God that a similar word could be spoken to many among our young people today, who appear to be satisfied to be copies of someone else.

It is never enough—whatever the gifts God has given—to be a copy; He needs originals. It takes courage, of course; but then, many of our young folk have more than we think.

In her book *You Learn By Living*, Eleanor Roosevelt has said this very thing that so badly needs saying in every generation. She had had her own struggles, but had won through, and was better qualified than most to encourage others. She was not only thinking of youth—thirty-year-olds like Ruth Draper, hesitating—but others of us further on, when she spoke of the 'pressures to live like our neighbours, to think like our community, to reshape ourselves in the image of someone else.' Summing-up, she added: 'It is a brave thing to have courage to be an individual . . . You have an obligation to be one.'

That was exactly how Ruth Draper came to think of life, her gifts, and what she might bring to the grand total. Beyond the power to work well with others, Henry James had put it for her once and for all: 'My dear child . . . you . . . have woven . . . your own . . . very beautiful . . . little Persian carpet . . . Stand on it!'

What many of us need, just where we are at this moment, is *the courage to stand*. Children love to play at being somebody else—and it is all right for them. But we are not children. We have no right to play neighbour, father, or circus man.

And don't let us imagine that this failure to be ourselves is limited to the female sex. It's not. Byron's admirers wore the same neck-tie; Melanchthon's students centuries before, had pushed through days with uneven shoulders, copying their master.

But can the Great Giver of Life ever be satisfied with this sort of thing?

Give me courage, O Lord, to face my lack of courage, here and now. Amen.

Carrying Seeds

It's fine to visit a far city, to serve in another country. Whether one travels by ship, plane, car or train, one tries to bring back to those unable to go something from where one has been—a toy Koala-bear from Sydney, a photo of the Queen's red-coated guards from London, small jingling cowbells from a mountain village in Switzerland.

But there are times when one brings back things without choosing them. A while ago, Mr A. J. Healy, of Lincoln College, New Zealand, found that Dr Godley, a botanist, had brought back with him a deposit of mud on his boots. But that was not the only reminder of his visit to Chile—in the mud were seeds. A sedge from South America, a tropical raspberry from New Caledonia, and an unnamed daisylike plant from Fiji, have been growing for some time at the college—all from seeds unwittingly brought back by travellers. Fitted with burrs or sharphooks, as well as the power to embed themselves in mud, they cling to hems of long coats, or drop secretly into men's trouser cuffs. They need no passports, no cash in pockets, or luggage labels.

And, of course, there are seeds of other kinds—one can pick up a smart word at a party, or place of business, and unknowingly bring home a weed; or one can pick up a new thought, and find to one's joy it's a flower. Human pride is but one exceptionally lusty seed, like unkindness, prejudice and spite. And wherever these sprout and spread, the world becomes a less lovely place.

Thirteen-year-old Henry Walker's experience with his engineer father, proved much more exciting. Together they tramped miles and miles over the hills and through the valleys of the Derbyshire Peak District, near their home. Mr Henry Walker—after whom his son was called—had been doing it for seventeen years at the time I'm thinking about. And it was a happy day when he could have company.

'We try to sow flowers in inaccessible spots,' said he, his eyes alight with the joy of it, 'and when it is time, we collect their seed to use again next year in another spot.'

Flowers of generosity, unselfishness, kindness, love, root well in the human heart and mind. There is a description of them in the New Testament—they are 'whatsoever things are true, whatsoever things are honest, whatsoever things are pure, whatsoever things are lovely, whatsoever things are of good report, full of virtue, and glad praise' (Phil. 4: 8).

Isaiah the prophet long ago dreamed of a day when all the weeds would be rooted out of the world, and only flowers and good trees remain. 'Instead,' he said—and isn't that a word to hold clearly in the heart—'instead of the thorn shall come up the fir tree, and instead of the briar shall come up the myrtle tree' (Isa. 55: 13). *Instead* of bad things, good things, *instead* of weeds, flowers. The thorn has long been the symbol of things useless and hurtful; but the purpose of God is life, beauty, goodness, truth, joy. The prophet dreams of a day when not only will good things be planted in the hearts and affairs of men—but bad things will be crowded out. 'Instead . . .' is his word from God.

It takes time—many of the firs and myrtles are but saplings yet; but we must not cease to believe in them. *The weeds are doomed.*

Let me this day, amid things difficult or dull, foolish or frustrating, keep my vision clear. Let Thy will be done in the world—and in my own life. Amen.

Either Way

WHAT fun it was! Do you remember when you first learned
to read? When you first learned to ride a bike? Think back!
'One thing which advancing years has brought us,' says
Naomi Jacob, in a chatty book of hers, 'is the pleasure of
looking back. Those tremendous days when things seemed
to happen suddenly. One day I couldn't read, the next I
was poring over Dickens in the big illustrated edition which
belonged to my mother. One day I was wobbling miserably
and apprehensively on my mother's bicycle—I remember it
was a 'Star' and I should imagine the heaviest machine in
existence—the next day I was careering wildly downhill, so
confident that I dared to take my feet off the pedals.'

I remember exactly; for it was that way with me—not
only in reading, and riding a bike—with lots of things. It
seemed a waste to dawdle—there were so many things to
discover, so much to do.

That is what made Mark's Gospel my first favourite—it
was a youthful story, full of those glorious words 'straightway' and 'immediately'. In by far the shortest of all four
gospels, those words occur almost thirty times. 'Straightway', the dictionary stood ready to assure me, meant
immediately (archaic); sometimes the word's meaning was
printed directly. Whilst a story-teller was usually satisfied
to have his story 'march', Mark rushed his on in breathless
haste; and as a child, I understood and welcomed that. One
moment Jesus was under the waters of the Jordan, the next
moment He was out. 'And straightway coming out of the
water, He saw the heavens opened' (Mark 1: 10). That's how
all the real things happened to me. Next, He was calling
His first disciples. 'And straightway they forsook their nets,
and followed Him' (Mark 1: 18). A sick woman pressed into

a crowd to touch the hem of His garment; next moment everything was changed for her. 'Straightway the fountain of her blood was dried up; and she felt in her body that she was healed . . . And Jesus, immediately knowing in Himself that virtue had gone out of Him, turned . . . and said, Who touched My clothes?' (Mark 5: 29–30). Both words are pressed into service to tell this dramatic happening. Each of these stories, and others as vivid, hasten into a place in Mark's Gospel.

And that seemed the perfectly natural way for things to happen, and to be recorded when I was first learning to read—Mark's Gospel among my Sunday books—and in no time riding a bicycle.

When later I heard Conversion spoken of as something that happened suddenly, it did not surprise me at all. It does now. Perhaps that means that I am getting further away from childhood. Dawn comes to some, I now see, with the suddenness of Paul's experience on the Damascus road. And there are many like him still. Dr C. S. Lewis, one of our finest Christian apologists and most widely read authors—his *Screwtape Letters*, *Problem of Pain* and others leaping into best-seller lists—tells us his experience. A typical twentieth-century agnostic, an Oxford don, he experienced a conversion whose suddenness Mark would have rejoiced in. 'I was driven to Whipsnade one Sunday morning. When we set out I did not believe that Jesus Christ was the Son of God, and when we reached the Zoo I did.'

But now I must also make room for the reality of another kind of awakening—a more gradual, gentle thing, as in the experience of Paul's young friend Timothy—*and no less real*.

Life—God be thanked—is Life either way!

O Lord, I will sing unto Thee a new song—one filled with praise! Amen.

No Tea Without Tea

TACT is a lovely thing—but it has its limitations. A twinkle in the eye of a friend seated beside her missionary husband clearly showed it to be so, as she told me of an experience in Fiji. The General Secretary for Overseas Missions was on a visit to the Indian Mission in Navua. At a given time the party set off down the coast in the Mission cutter. Things went well. After a while, the missionary, not knowing that the foodbox had been left behind, asked the distinguished visitor if he would like a cup of tea. Yes, he replied, the sea air and sun had given him a thirst. The houseboy was sent to prepare it. The primus was lit; but when the water was nearly boiled, the boy put his head out of the cabin, and said, 'Sa sega Saka na sucu.' (There is no milk, Sir.) This sad news was passed on to the guest, who with good grace, agreed to drink it without.

A few minutes later, a sense of expectation was interrupted by a second appearance of the boy, to report, 'Sa sega Saka na suka.' (Sir, we have no sugar.) This was also communicated to the guest, who by this time was really ready for his tea—without milk or sugar.

The primus still buzzing merrily, another minute passed; then the boy appeared a third time, to report in a dejected voice, 'Sa sega Saka na Ti.' (Sir, we have no tea.)

'At least,' commented my friend, '*he was tactful*, and kept the worst news until the last!'

But I must be more realistic. *You can't have tea without tea*—that is plain enough; *and you can't have Life without the Lord of Life*. 'He that hath the Son hath life,' saith John, 'and he that hath not the Son of God hath not life' (I John 5: 12). There is no mistaking his meaning. And yet, so many seem to miss it—to think that as long as they are law-abiding, decent and friendly, they can have *Christianity without Christ.* Surely they are not even interested in Christianity?

John—in that early band of disciples—knew what they were, and what they were up against in the world of that time in which they were called to witness; and he knew that decent ideas were not enough. Even Christ's teaching alone could not create Christianity—it had to be centred in His Person; and more than that, in His Risen Person. It was only after the darkness of sin and death had been scattered, and the stone rolled away from the grave, that John could testify to the glory of that triumph.

Andrew Young, poet in our day, gathers up that dynamic essential in words unforgettable. Says he:

> *I was not blind and yet He gave me sight;*
> *I was not deaf and yet He gave me hearing;*
> *Nor was I dead, yet me He raised to life.*

And men and women are still entering into that experience. 'Facing the Risen Christ,' says Dorothy Sayers, with her rare powers of revealing the central clue, 'the disciples *could now go and do something about the problem of sin and suffering.* They had seen the strong hands of God twist the crown of thorns into a crown of glory, and in hands as strong as that they knew themselves safe.'

In Him, and in Him alone is Life! There is no tea without tea; and there is no Life without the Lord of Life!

O God, my Father, I bless Thee for the fellowship of those who follow Christ today. Above all, I bless Thee for showing me Thy life-giving power and purpose, in Him, my Saviour and Lord. Amen.

Self-starters

I MAY be mistaken. But the world, it seems to me, has more and more motors with self-starters—but fewer people. A need arises, a good cause waits to be served—but how few can do anything without a committee? Some efforts have to be organized if money and energy are to be conserved—but not all, surely. In the Welfare State, the United Nations, and ecumenical Church, there is danger of personal responsibility being swamped.

I think of Peter the disciple, in this regard—after the Denial, Crucifixion, and Resurrection. He returned from fishing with his friends, to find a fire of coals burning, and a fish breakfast laid thereon; and more wonderful even than that, to be offered presently, the forgiveness of his Lord. 'Simon, son of Jonas,' he is asked three times, 'lovest thou Me?' And three times he answers, declaring his love—and three times is told what to do next. One might have thought that experience enough for the moment, but no; catching sight of John, Peter asks: 'What shall this man do?' Jesus—the moment past, so tender—tells him pretty straightly, to get on with his own job: 'What is that to thee? Follow thou Me.'

And isn't that a word many of us need to hear? Whatever the other fellow does, *we have a personal responsibility in the presence of our Lord*. That is what I like so much about the story behind a church I passed by, haversack on back, down in Cornwall. Now the minister of Wesley Church, Liskeard, has written to me.

Wesley preached in Liskeard; and years before his death, the first 'preaching house' was established, 'a low thatched outhouse.' Twenty years later, it was replaced by a chapel, and forty years on, by another. Then, one night, while still only four years in use, a disastrous fire burned it down. The people, with what limited means they had, fought the flames, but in the morning nothing remained but bare black walls—and the splendid sense of personal responsibility of those who worshipped in that place. There is not the least doubt about that—proof is in the story of two boys, Henry Lucas and Andrew Kingston. They held a 'solemn meeting' between themselves, and resolved '*that we give all we can, and beg all we can . . . and that we begin at once.*' (Note the inspired order of procedure.) And then each headed his collecting-book with all that he had: 'Master Henry £20. and Master Andrew £18.'

Little wonder that within four months, the foundation-stone of the present building was laid!

Is there anything today to make-up for such a personal sense of responsibility? Nothing, that I know of. Happily, there are many still in our day—unknown, known—who can match it. They do not say: 'What shall this man do?' or, 'If I were you . . .' One by one, in the presence of their Living Lord, they take up the challenge. So little Japanese Kagawa, moves down into a filthy hovel in the slums; young Dr Howard Somervell, after a thrilling attempt on Everest, stays to minister in a mission hospital—since overlooking personal responsibility, he can never again look into the eyes of his Lord, or say prayers to Him; and Jane Addams sets herself to clean up Chicago's West Side, by opening the friendly door of 'T' ole Hull House' on Halstead Street, that the poor Italians thereabout come to call 'The House of God'.

That is how so many good things happen! *We need more self-starters!*

Thou who art the beginning and ending of all things good, number me this day, I beg of Thee, in the honourable company of Thy true servants. Amen.

Learning

Do you remember when you first learned to tell the time? It's a long way back now; but it was an important moment in growing-up. The hands of the watch, the clock suddenly spelled sense. And up-risings and down-sittings—to charge the Psalmist's words with additional meaning—have been subject to that discovery ever since. Only an Edison—independent in so many ways—dare say to a boy, 'Never look at the clock!' For the rest of us, 'Tick! tock! tick! tock!' spells out the tyranny of Time.

Harold Monro, in our day, feels a responsibility to face us with this fact. Says he—

> When first you learn to read the clock
> That moment you are in a snare,
> Doomed for the rest of life to stand
> A victim to that patient hand.

Few at any time, I feel, accomplish more than the ministerial founder of the *British Weekly*, Dr Robertson Nicoll; but he hated clocks. 'I particularly dislike,' said he, 'people who profess to be busy, and seem to be hurried, people who look at the clock when you visit them, or when they visit you.'

We can try to disguise the fact in any one of a dozen ways we've discovered, but there is no doubt—when good manners have done what they can—that clocks tie us all a little anxiously to the passing moment.

A while ago, Princeton University announced that it had restored a very unusual clock, acquired away back in 1771, called the Rittenhouse Orery. In addition to showing the motions of the heavenly bodies according to Newton's system, it told the time, *not only by the hours, but by the centuries!*

It's a pity that this kind of clock is so uncommon—we could each do with one. A great many things that we hesitate to do might be done, if only we could see them against the centuries; and a great many things we fuss about now, might as well be left undone. 'The secret of life,' Emerson was fond of saying, 'is to set the hours against the centuries.'

But how are we to do it? Our Lord somehow managed to see life in its proper perspective. We never read of Him being anxious, hurrying, or fretting. He saw men doing these very things everywhere—one building bigger barns to house his overflowing harvest of the moment, others so intent on testing a piece of land, attending to the wants of a wife, trying out a team of oxen that they missed the royal banquet, life. 'What shall it profit a man,' He asked, 'if he gain the whole world, and lose his own soul?' (Mark 8: 36).

The centuries have proved His values right. As Lecomte du Nouy sees it in our day: 'The Roman patricians of the year 33, the philosophers, and the intellectuals would have been highly amused if they had been told that the unknown young Jew, tried by the procurator of a distant colony . . . would play an infinitely greater role than Caesar, would dominate the history of the Occident, and become the purest symbol of all humanity.'

> *Strange is it not! The Caesars pass,*
> *Shorn of their power and pride.*
> *While He, the lowly-born is King,*
> *Whom once they crucified!*

Daily, O Lord, trivial things of little value press in upon me. Grant me a truer perspective—give me patience to wait Thy good time, and a glad trust. Amen.

How Old is Old Age?

THE Competition craze keeps spreading, till now it reaches every corner of our life. The local foodmarket wants a slogan for its new line in toothpaste; the zoo wants a name for its baby hippo; and now the local bank has a pile of forms ready for what it calls 'a bumper competition, with sixty lovely prizes'. Open to children and adults, each depositor is asked to select six answers from a list of twelve, and set down in order of importance 'my reasons for saving'.

I suppose it is a competition as sensible as any; but I couldn't help smiling when I heard of the entry of one competitor—an old lady of ninety-four. 'My reason for saving,' she said, '*is for my old age!*'

Well, who can say that that isn't an answer as good as any? The point is who can say when old age sets in? Only one thing is certain, we are all living longer these days. Whether that is a good thing remains to be seen. Plato argued that the disciples of Hippocrates were guilty of a serious mischief if by their healing art they enabled any to live on beyond their span of usefulness. Petrarch took up this same argument in his turn, and many another has echoed it since.

But one would be blind not to notice how widely the span of usefulness differs. Nearing seventy, Corot, the great painter, was overheard to say eagerly: 'If God spares me for another ten years, I think I may still learn to paint.' Kant was seventy-four when he wrote his monumental work *Metaphysics of Ethics*; Goethe was past eighty when he finished *Faust*; Cato learned Greek at eighty. And there are any number in our own day to keep these company— famous names, many of them—Sir Winston Churchill, Lord Russell, Mother Moses, the artist, not to mention others less distinguished, we ourselves know personally. 'When one ceases to be curious about things,' one has said, 'old age is upon him.'

Old age, as I see it, isn't something that descends when one reaches a certain age, produces a double chin, or when one becomes eligible for a pension; it's rather something that's woven out of all the years. But it is a time which has special needs. Good health helps, without a doubt; a multitude of interests begun in youth and middle-age and carried through the years; money enough to meet one's modest needs; but above all, it's a matter of spirit.

The shrewdest piece of self-knowledge I have come across, is that which shows through the prayer of an old Roman Catholic Mother Superior: 'Lord, Thou knowest better than I know myself that I am growing older and will some day be old. Keep me from getting talkative, and particularly from the fatal habit of thinking I must say something on every subject and on every occasion. Release me from craving to straighten out everybody's affairs. Keep my mind free from the recital of endless details—give me wings to get to the point. I ask for grace enough to listen to the tales of others' pains. Help me to endure them with patience. But seal my lips on my own aches and pains—they are increasing and my love of rehearsing them is becoming sweeter as the years go by. Teach me the glorious lesson that occasionally it is possible that I may be mistaken. Keep me reasonably sweet; I do not want to be a saint—some of them are so hard to live with—but a sour old woman is one of the crowning works of the devil. Make me thoughtful, but not moody; helpful, but not bossy. With my vast store of wisdom, it seems a pity not to use it all—but Thou knowest Lord, that I want a few friends at the end. Amen.'

Give Thy holy joy and courage, O God, to all who find their years mounting and strength diminishing. Amen.

A Tribute

THE whole world round we have again been faced with the implications of a rich partnership—*a great woman standing behind a great man.* 'My marriage,' wrote Sir Winston Churchill in an autobiography, 'was much the most fortunate and joyous event which happened to me in the whole of my life, for what can be more glorious than to be united in one's way through life with a being incapable of an ignoble thought.'

What greater tribute can a man pay to his wife? 'Clemmie', now seventy-nine, has provided all through momentous years the kind of background so needful to a man in leadership—indeed, to any man—playing the roles of wife, confidante, hostess and mother, with serenity, efficiency and grace. It has not been easy; for the couple have lived through turbulent experiences. On days of big debates in the House of Commons—through peace and war—Sir Winston liked to see his 'Clemmie' in the ladies' gallery. As he rose to speak, his gaze was always lifted to where she sat, answering with a discreet movement of a hand. And in a score of other private and public situations he depended on her as well—his faith in her as his closest critic was unbounded.

The free world that owes so much to Sir Winston, owes not less to the woman who provided his constant background.

She has not been alone in this, of course; she follows an honourable pattern. There is an old proverb that it takes four women to make a decent man—his mother, his wife, his sister and his daughter. One thing is unquestioned: his wife stands in a unique relationship—if she will. We don't need to go back beyond the period of our own lifetime to hear echoes of this tribute. Lord Southwood, chairman of

Odhams Press, prominent in philanthropic work, the Great Ormond Street Hospital for Sick Children, and numerous other benevolent causes, wrote: 'No words of mine can express my gratitude for the wonderful love and devotion of my dear wife. Her guidance and her infinite patience through all the years we have been united have been something more beautiful than words can express.'

There is that same superlative note—and in no sense, recklessly or thoughtlessly used. For these two husbands daily handled words with care, and telling effectiveness, as part of their public ministry.

To add the word of another of our day, serving in a public way—Field-Marshall Jan Smuts, the great South African statesman, is to hear the same tribute echoed, if not in classical words. Paying tribute to his wife on the day of their golden wedding, he delighted to say: 'She is the steam in my kettle.'

With Sir Winston Churchill, these two husbands moved constantly in the public eye—and their wives likewise; but there are countless humble men, performing every day essential work the world round, who know that they handle but half their task, the remainder becomes possible because of the woman who stands behind them. And richly blessed is that community, that country where this relationship ordained of God, is many times multiplied. This is as good a time as any to remind ourselves of these essential values.

History has a way of glossing over shining personal contributions. When somebody talked at length of the Pilgrim Fathers, their courage, their cares, their qualities of leadership, someone interjected, 'What about the Pilgrim Mothers?' The speaker, a little taken aback, replied, 'But what had they to put up with?' 'Well, to start with,' came the answer, 'the Pilgrim Fathers!'

We marvel, O Lord, that Thou hast put into our human hands the issues of life. Amen.

Gullible Grown-ups

THERE are people—no great distance from any one of us—who will *swallow anything*. Given time, one advertising agent claimed lately that he could induce the public to eat sawdust instead of cereal for breakfast. And I don't doubt him, if the vitamin content could be underlined.

Newspapers are full of advertisements from those who know this. 'Use the right bath soap,' they say, 'Smoke the right cigarette,' 'Drive the right car,' and 'charm will be yours, prestige, business success.' And these 'amazing secrets' are repeated in seductive tones over radio, on TV, visualized during every interval at the cinema, and pasted to confront us on every hoarding. It costs immense sums—as the protomers know—but it's worth it all. *Somebody will swallow it whole!*

Tourism knows this gullibility in human-nature, too. Guides can be unashamedly glib. Drawing on experience, during a BBC Brains Trust, Commander A. B. Campbell confessed with a chuckle: 'I conducted a party of twenty-three American college girls round Europe for forty-three days. When we got to Stratford-on-Avon, I found that two or three of them were infected with the Baconian theory, and that nothing could convince them that the man who wrote Shakespeare's plays was none other than William Shakespeare. I decided that if I could not stop them believing this Baconian nonsense, I would at least stop them talking about it. So I asked: "Do you know that it was Shakespeare that wrote the Psalms?"

'"What on earth do you mean, Commander?" they shouted.

'"Well," I replied, "you will know that Shakespeare died when he was 46 and wrote 46 plays and 46 sonnets."

'Nobody was well enough informed to contradict me.

'"Now if you will look up Psalm 46," I continued, "you will find that the 46th word from the beginning is 'shake' and the 46th word from the end, omitting Selah which is not part of the Psalm, is 'spear'. What more convincing proof can you need?"'

You smile? But have you never yourself bought a religious book from a man on your own doorstep, with a story as gullible? If not—then you have never got as far as listening to the 'line of talk' offered by well-spoken, well-tailored young Mormons, or door-to-door visitors under the banner of 'Jehovah's Witnesses'.

If we only knew deeply the things of our Faith; if we studied our New Testament as eagerly as a number of other things, this couldn't happen. We wouldn't be in danger of swallowing the first bit of religious 'sales talk' we opened our door to meet. In this day of classes, study groups, and good authoritive paperback books in plenty, there is no excuse. We buy cook books, travelbooks, handbooks on Russian, Spanish, Yogi, family-planning, and atomic physics—why not a decent religious book by an outstanding Christian, written in the language that we ordinary people know?

It is easy to smile; but gullible grown-ups—especially those of us calling ourselves 'Christian'—have no right to *feel* our religion, and not *think* it.

'To think, and to think hard,' says Professor Jessop, in *Effective Religion*—good title—'is a paramount religious duty. Only when we fulfil this duty will God's illimitable resources be made available to us.'

O Living Lord, let the place where I live, and those amongst whom I work, be enriched by my thought. Give me the courage to seek out Thy will, this day, and do it; to follow after Thy truth, and love it. Amen.

So Personal

I AM sorry for Johnny—as I was several times sorry for myself, when obliged to mouth Aboriginal names when in Australia's burning heart. Johnny's name, till lately—Johnny Jambijimba—proved impossibly difficult for some. It was misspelt, and mispronounced; what was even more distressing, his occasional letters went astray. Some he never recovered. So now he has given notice in the local newspaper that he is changing his name—henceforth it will be Johnny Jambijimba-Yannarilyi!

Delightful! Let us hope it works out. Johnny might be called on to think of a simpler solution.

One thing is certain, *a name is such a personal possession*—it makes no difference whether one lives in Alice Springs, Bishop Auckland, or New York. Numbers serve in some situations—but they are very impersonal.

Joseph Conrad faced Johnny's problem in his own setting. Baptized Josef Teodor Konrad Nalecz Korzeniowski at birth in Poland, all was well till he began writing in English, and became a distinguished man of letters. Then something had to be done about his name, if it was not to be mutilated, or worse, dropped for a number. He changed it to Joseph Conrad.

Few of us have to face this problem. We may grow up caring little for the names bestowed on us at baptism—I'm not over fond of my own, a diminutive of Margarita—but such names, with time, seem to take on a certain 'fittingness'. They are so very personal.

At one time, when people lived in small villages and compact communities gathered round a great house, castle, or master, a Christian name was sufficient—a situation common in Britain up to the Norman Conquest. When the population increased greatly, so that in one village there might be three or four Johns, each name was tied to a trade, master or location. John who thatched became John the thatcher, his neighbour John the miller, till with time the article 'the' was dropped, and the first man became John Thatcher, the other John Miller.

Bible names introduced a certain flavour—some of them seeming to us in this age, very quaint—Cabel, Theophilus, Barak, Deborah, Asaph. Mary and John, in time, established themselves as prime favourites—a position they have not since surrendered, though Ann, Elizabeth, Peter and David now run them a close second. It's hard to think what parents had in mind when bestowing some of the odd names appearing in the current register, Ecamilia, Izma, Balon. The last may well be a family name used in a Christian sense. Whatever the choice, there is something very personal about one's name. Dr Fosdick, the beloved writer and preacher of Riverside Church, sees in this fact something very special in this day when in countless ways in our busy, bustling, impersonal world, individuals are likely to be overlooked. God is our Father—and the essential of true fatherhood is an individual relationship. 'He lifts us up,' says the Doctor, wonderingly, 'from the obscurity of our littleness; He picks us out from the multitude of our fellows, He gives to our lives the dignity of His individual care. The Eternal God calls us every one by name. He is not the God of mankind in the mass; He is the God of Abraham, of Isaac, and of Jacob.'

No wonder the Bible—recording His promises, His laws, and His dealings with men and women—is full of ' Thou's' and ' Me's'!

O God, I rejoice that Thou art not only infinitely great—but intimately near. Amen.

My Bank

A LIGHT came into the eyes of my bank-manager this morning, as I opened my wallet. Cheques drawn on a Maori Bank are very rare. The existence of No. 47. in the family treasures of a friend of mine proved of great interest—I placed a traced copy before him. Impressively printed, as nearly as possible like a European cheque—bearing Na Ingiki Tawhiao's name—it was drawn for five hundred pounds.

Five hundred pounds, of course, was a great sum of money in pioneer days. The land waited to be cleared and cultivated, settlements were few and scattered, roads between them almost non-existent.

The Maoris were not slow to observe that English settlers drew money from a Bank—each using a cheque-book. Ready to copy anything that spelt advance, it was no time before a Maori Bank appeared.

But there was one important point that hadn't been fully grasped—that *one could only get money out, if he had put money in*. Elementary, of course, but the whole idea of banking was at the time. So the cheque under discussion was never honoured. And the Maori Bank lasted only a short time!

Intervening years have made Maoris as knowledgeable in these matters as any of us. But there are realms where still we expect to get something for nothing. Take *friendship*. It is common to hear one or another say he is neglected and lonely. Few take any notice of his plight. Some who complain thus are old—but not all. One and a half million people in Britain today live alone—which is not to say that one and a half million are lonely. Far from it. Many live this way from choice. Loneliness is not wholly a matter of proximity, any more than is friendship. The fact behind the complaint is more often that in a relationship that might have yielded friendship, *they have tried to take something out without putting anything in.*

The same applies in *travel*. The 'good traveller' concerns himself with more than travel sickness pills, and luggage labels. It is a waste, in John Gunther's words—author of the famous 'Inside books'—'to strike a country cold.' *You've got to put something in*—a background of planning, studied facts, listed points of interest, history, human characteristics. 'It will be acknowledged that travelling is attended with pleasure and profit,' to quote an early traveller, 'but it is no less certain that these advantages cannot be obtained without paying.' Exactly!

And the same is true of our *worship*—though this essential is often overlooked. The preacher is not in the pulpit to do something *for* us, but something *with* us. Worship is a corporate act. It is surprising that some confess that they don't 'get much out of it'?

Says one, more honest than most of us—

> *Back to the church of my fathers, I went—*
> *The years away had been long—*
> *Seeking an accrual of faith*
> *To make my spirit strong.*
> *I looked about me and I saw*
> *Humble, devout folk there . . .*
> *But no fund of faith was there for me,*
> *Only emptiness and doubt;*
> *For years I had put nothing in—*
> *What could I hope to draw out?*

Merciful Lord, if I have taken good gifts from life, without a lively sense of responsibility, forgive me. Hear my prayer, and let my cry come unto Thee. Amen.

168

Going Back . . .

THE audacity of that little three-masted wooden tub, *Terra Nova*, has long been touched with glory. Sacrifice of life, unfinished journals and letters, and a few superb pictures of ice and snow have fastened the name Antarctica in our memory forever.

In the New Zealand port of Lyttelton lives an old fellow of eighty-four who went south with Captain Scott. He is the oldest survivor of the expedition. He has just been back—and has been telling me of it. Mr McCarthy 'has enjoyed every minute of it,' he assures me. 'It has been a wonderful experience after fifty-two years.'

Amazed at the progress in the south, he says, 'towns are being built there. Tourists will be going to the Antarctic in a few years, for skating and winter sports.'

Outstanding in his memories was the launch excursion and time ashore at Cape Hallet, and recognition of the ease of travel helicopters have brought to the great white spaces. In the very nature of things, a return trip of the kind Mr McCarthy has just completed, was fraught with danger for an eighty-four-year-old. I do not mean that life aboard the supply freighter was disagreeable—far from it; or that he ran the risk of being worn out, or lost in a blizzard—far from it. The hazards of returning after fifty-two years were largely in the mind.

Long before men dreamed of the white spaces of Antarctica, or thought of going there, they used to sing a song about 'Gwine back to Dixie'—and many of us, in our turn, learned it. Warm with nostalgia, it allowed a brief escape from things as they were; it held the power to bridge distances, it was full of a strange loyalty to former days. *And there its danger lay*. For it is always dangerous to go 'back to

Dixie', call it what you will—the street where one's childhood was spent, the church where one's religion first became real, or Antarctica.

Geography has little to do with this, really—though places change with the years, and people change. Unless one faces up to these facts realistically, a return trip is bound to be disappointing. It can't be otherwise—growing towns take the place of exploration huts, helicopter travel that of tiresome tugging at loaded sledges. No place—Dixie, Antarctica—ever stays still, except in dreams. And all unknowingly, one has changed, too—to be older, more mature in one's judgement, wider in experience. As well, the years tend to distil from Dixie only such drops of satisfaction as one is prepared to receive—after so long a time, Dixie seems the most pleasant place, the company finer, the sky overhead of a crystal clearness found nowhere else. And in this lies the danger of 'going back'—not only to a *place*, but also to an *experience*. Few of us are as realistic about this, as old Mr McCarthy was.

The Psalmist looked back to a day when God was as real as the breath in a strong man's lungs. 'Marvellous things did He,' are his words, 'in the land of Egypt, in the field of Zoan.' Exactly! And it is good to keep them in remembrance—but what about *now?* It is good to recount one's early religious experience, with, 'O happy day that fixed my choice'—but what about *today?* Our Lord's penetrating question is: 'Do ye now believe?' (John 16: 31). In the most real sense, religion rests not alone on what God once did, *but on what He now does*, not alone on what Christ was, but on *what He now is.*

Gracious Lord, let my religion be an experience in the present tense. Amen.

Acknowledgements

My thanks are due to the following for permission to quote
from copyright works: Macmillan & Co. Ltd. for an extract
from *Testament of Friendship* by Vera Brittain; Condé Nast
Publications Ltd. for the reported speech of Christopher Fry;
and the Editor of the *British Weekly* for material which first
appeared in his publication.